Taking You Home

Taking You Home

poems and conversations

Derick Thomson
Iain Crichton Smith
& Andrew Mitchell

Gaelic translation of Taking You Home
Myles Campbell

ARGYLL ✠ PUBLISHING

© Poetry: Derick Thomson,
  Carcanet Press for Iain Crichton Smith,
  Andrew Mitchell
© Voice transcriptions: Derick Thomson,
  Estate of Iain Crichton Smith
© Photographs: Julian May, Andrew Mitchell

First published 2006

Argyll Publishing
Glendaruel
Argyll PA22 3AE
Scotland
www.argyllpublishing.com

The authors have asserted their moral rights.

British Library Cataloguing-in-Publication Data.
A catalogue record for this book is available from the British Library.

ISBN 1 902831 51 9

The publisher acknowledges subisdy from the Scottish Arts Council towards the publication of this volume.

Scottish
Arts Council

Cover Photo
At the Stones of Callanish by Andrew Mitchell, National Portrait Gallery, London, exhibited in 2000, also in the collections of National Library of Scotland and Scottish Poetry Library.

Printing
Bell & Bain Ltd, Glasgow

With thanks to Julian May, Senior Arts Producer at the
BBC, who made this journey possible,
for his company along the way and his production of the
Kaleidoscope Feature, 'How Many Miles From Bayble?'
broadcast on BBC Radio 4, 26th August 1995.

ACKNOWLEDGEMENTS

Special thanks to: Donalda Henderson, Derick Thomson,
Ian MacDonald for continual support for the project and
help with Gaelic and English texts.
Thanks to: Stewart Conn, Gary Geddes, Douglas Gifford,
Sandy Hutchison, Holger Klein, Ronnie Renton,
Nancy McGuire.
Financial Support: the author wishes to thank the
following bodies for their funding support: Scottish Arts
Council; Gaelic Society of Inverness.

Three poets on the beach

CONTENTS

INTRODUCTION

T HE ISLAND of Lewis, for long recognised as the
birthplace of intrepid sailors, theologians, Gaelic singers
of great renown and, of course, countless academics in many
disciplines, has a long and distinguished cultural history.
Throughout many centuries, the island has produced a great
company of illustrious individuals, among them the medieval
Lawmen of Ness under the Lordship of the Isles, the Blind
Poet and Harper of Dunvegan Castle, and in more recent
times Alexander Mackenzie, the explorer whose name is
enshrined on the map of Canada. Modern artists inherit the
memories of their achievements. But much more immediate
are the pressures of events: Clearances, emigration, political
controversy and the dissenting fervour of Evangelical
Christianity. All of these, one way or another, have left subtle
traces in the writings of Derick Thomson and Iain Crichton
Smith.

Like other parts of Gaelic Scotland, Lewis has two forms
of its name: *Leòdhas* is its Gaelic eponym. Gaelic men and
women, too, enjoy the same double nomenclature – a legacy
bestowed by a linguistic army of occupation. This is a decisive
inheritance, obviously, for biculturalism can offer a writer a
powerful challenge. Equally obviously, it can be a source of
rich experience, depending as it does on the creative vigour
of the individual. The writers whose work this book celebr-
ates have all drawn on two worlds.

Ruaraidh MacThòmais/Derick Thomson and *Iain Mac
a' Ghobhainn*/Iain Crichton Smith, both raised near one
another, are strikingly different. In part this is a token of the
richness of contemporary Gaelic writing. It also involves
writing in English by native Gaels. As a poet, Iain's greatest
contribution is in English; what he brought to Gaelic

9

literature, superbly, is a wonderfully flexible, innovative style of prose in novel and short story alike. Derick, the outstanding scholar writing in both languages, is the major Gaelic poet of the second half of the twentieth century. What links the two men is their rejection of the provincial. Solidly rooted in their native community, they have in different ways seen and realised the universal in the particular.

Their family backgrounds were culturally rich in somewhat contrastive modes. Derick's father was a poet of distinction; his mother a sweet singer of age-old songs. Iain's mother, a woman of intense Christian faith, had an outstanding eloquence in the expression of religious experience.

Andrew Mitchell, stimulated and inspired by the poets' conversation and their poetry, has added a whole new dimension to our appreciation of their work. Very appropriately, he has done so in his own poetry, and these poems also are a memorable achievement. Finally, to round off a remarkable book, Myles Campbell has turned Andrew's poems into idiomatic Gaelic which is not only true to the original but is also cast in a contemporary style in which his own characteristic poetic voice can be heard. That, too, is impressively successful.

John MacInnes

THE BAYBLE POETS

NEITHER of the Bayble poets was born in the village on the island of Lewis. Derick Thomson was born in Stornoway in 1921, moving to Bayble as a small child when his father, the Gaelic scholar and poet James Thomson, was appointed headmaster at Bayble School in 1922. Iain Crichton Smith was born in Glasgow in 1928. He also moved to Bayble when he was a small child. Iain's father was ill with tuberculosis, which

Derick Thomson and Iain Crichton Smith on Bayble beach

killed him when Iain was two or three years old. This produced both the straitened financial circumstances of Iain's childhood (he was the middle child of three brothers) and his mother's consistent fears about the boy's tendency to bronchitis. As a result he missed a lot of school, but did manage to play football for the village team.During community work, cutting peats or harvesting, for instance, he might as easily be found reading a book in a quiet corner.

Both poets came to work principally in what was their second language: Derick's first language being English and Iain's Gaelic. The difference in age between them meant they were not close friends as children, though they knew one another because of the nature of village life and also because Derick was a friend of Iain's older brother, John Alex.

Their educational paths were very similar: Bayble School, the Nicolson Institute in Stornoway and the University of Aberdeen. It was at university their paths began to diverge. Derick undertook further study in Cambridge and Bangor, which strengthened his knowledge of Celtic cultures. Years later he was to surprise Welsh poets at an international reading by delivering one of his own poems translated into faultless Welsh. Iain concentrated more on English and Latin.

Both had to undergo military service. Iain spent two years of National Service in the Army Education Corps. Derick served during the Second World War in the Royal Air Force, being posted for part of that time back to Lewis, where his duties involved climbing to the top of radar masts to service them in all weathers.

After World War II, Derick successively taught at the Universities of Edinburgh, Glasgow and Aberdeen, before being appointed as Professor of Celtic at the University of Glasgow in 1963. He had already founded the all-Gaelic quarterly *Gairm* in 1952, and established the associated Gairm Publications as a publishing house from 1958. The magazine *Gairm* continued until its 200th issue in 2002.

Iain was initially appointed to teach at Clydebank High School, from where he used to go to Helensburgh with his mother, to listen to the sound of the sea. He remained at Oban High School, his next teaching post, for the rest of his teaching career until retirement in 1977. Iain wrote throughout his teaching career both in Gaelic and English, retiring to devote himself to full-time writing, and moving to Taynuilt in 1980 with his wife Donalda.

There was much contact between both poets over the years. Derick frequently published Iain's Gaelic poems in *Gairm*. Initially Iain had shown some of his early poems to Derick, and it was only later the older poet came to realise with horror that Iain was throwing away those poems not receiving praise! The speed Iain worked at and his prolific output were almost legendary. He wrote the novel *Consider the Lilies* in a two-week school holiday. Whilst viewing a Gaelic play, he remarked to Donalda, 'I'm really enjoying this play. The writer has my sense of humour. Who wrote it?' 'You did, Iain,' she replied. Iain died of cancer in 1998, aged seventy. Derick is eighty-five at the time of writing.

Both poets effectively left Lewis when they went to university at seventeen, but their island childhood experiences formed a core to their lifelong creative work.

POEMS BY DERICK THOMSON

Pabail

Air iomall an talamh-àitich, eadar dhà sholas,
tha a' churracag a' ruith 's a' stad, 's a' ruith 's a' stad,
is cobhar bàn a broillich, mar rionnag an fheasgair,
ga lorg 's ga chall aig mo shùilean,
is tùis an t-samhraidh
ga lorg 's ga chall aig mo chuinnlean,
is fras-mhullach tonn an t-sonais
ga lorg 's ga chall aig mo chuimhne.

Bàgh Phabail fodham, is baile Phabail air fàire,
sluaisreadh sìorraidh a' chuain, a lorg 's a shireadh
eadar clachan a' mhuil 's an eag nan sgeir,
is fo ghainmhich a' gheodha,
gluasad bithbhuan a' bhaile, am bàs 's an ùrtan,
an ùrnaigh 's an t-suirghe, is mìle cridhe
ag at 's a' seacadh, is ann an seo
tha a' churracag a' ruith 's a' stad, 's a' ruith 's a' stad.

Bayble

On the edge of the arable land, between two lights,
the plover runs and stops, and runs and stops,
the white foam of its breast like the star of evening,
discovered and lost in my looking,
and the fragrance of summer,
discovered and lost by my nostrils,
and the topmost grains of the wave of content,
discovered and lost by my memory.

Bayble Bay below me, and the village on the skyline,
the eternal action of the ocean, its seeking and searching
between the pebble stones and in the rock crannies,
and under the sand of the cove;
the everlasting movement of the village,
death and christening, praying and courting,
and a thousand hearts swelling and sinking, and here,
the plover runs and stops, and runs and stops.

Chaill mi mo chridhe riut

Chaill mi mo chridhe riut ann an toiseach Màigh,
bha do shliasaid blàth,
teann, mìn, 's ged a b' òigh thu
bha do chìochan làn,
bòidheach fon t-sròl uaine;
agus ann an Og-mhìos nan uan
laigh mi air t' uachdar,
's cha robh thu air do thruailleadh;
is an uair a thàinig Iuchar
dh'fhaoisgneadh na lusan
is thàinig blàth air a' chanach;
ach thàinig a sin am bruaillean
is fras air na gruaidhean
is mas robh fhios agam dè chanainn
thàinig an lìth donn air a raineach,
's cha robh a chridh agam na chanadh
gun do chaill mi sìoda mìn a' chanaich.

I lost my heart to you

I lost my heart to you at the start of May,
your thighs were warm,
firm and smooth, and though you were a maid
your breasts were full,
beautiful beneath green satin;
and in the lambs' month June
I lay upon you,
and you were not defiled;
and when July came
the buds of the plants burst open
and bloom came on the cotton grass;
but then came anxiety
and tears on cheeks,
and before I knew what to say
a brown tint spread over the bracken,
and I could not say – I had not the heart to do it –
that I had lost the smooth silk of the cotton grass.

Nuair a thilleas mi

Nuair a thilleas mi
bidh 'm bàrr-gùg air a' bhuntàt',
bidh 'n t-seillean a' crònan,
bidh bhò a' muathal gu eadradh
nuair a thilleas mi.

Nuair a ruigeas mi,
a' breith air làimh oirbh,
bidh fuachd na fàinne
air deàrn' an dòchais
nuair a ruigeas mi.

Nuair a laigheas mi
an com do charthannais,
thig an gug-gùg
's an o-draochan maille ris
an uair a laigheas mi.

'S an uair a dh'èireas mi
air a' mhadainn ud,
bidh 'n fhàinne sgealbt'
is a' bhò gun bhainn' aice,
's an t-eilean riabhach mar bu chiad aithne dhomh.

When I come back

When I come back
the potato flowers will be out,
the bees humming,
the cows lowing to milking
when I come back.

When I arrive,
shaking you by the hand,
the coldness of the ring
will be on the palm of hope
when I arrive.

When I lie down
in your kind breast,
the cuckoo will come
and wailing with it,
when I lie down.

And when I rise
on that morning,
the ring will be shattered
and the cow dry
and the dark-brown island as I first knew it.

Geodha air chùl na grèine

Tha fèath air a' bhàgh a-nochd, 's an sruth dol thar na maoile;
cobhar air a' chreig bhàite, is falpanaich air stalla,
gàir aig an tonn tha fad ás, is siubhal dian aig na cuantan,
ach tha 'n cuan tha seo 'na thàmh gun bhàt' aig cala.

Far na chladhaich e linne rèidh le an-shocair nan làithean,
geodha air chùl na grèine, 's a mhol gun ghrùid,
far an rachadh bliannachan geal na gealaich seachad siar air,
air chuthach, gun iaradh, a' sireadh ceann-uidhe gun ùidh.

Thrèig am bradan an cuan ann an linn a' bhàigh chiùin seo,
a' lorg na h-aibhne òig ud, 's nan gluaiste clach
reubadh beithir airgeadach beò a' ghliocais 's an eòlais
uisgeachan balbha criostail nan sgarbh 's nan lach.

Tha leac an seo air an tràigh far am biodh na mnathan a' feitheamh
nan eathraichean beaga iasgaich nuair thigeadh sian;
is tric a bha ulaidh a' chridhe is ulaidh a' chuain ás an aonais,
is a gheibheadh iad blas dearg a' bhradain searbh air am beul.

Gu tric 'nan seasamh a' coimhead na mara far na chailleadh an cuid,
's 'nan suidh' anns na taighean san d'fhuair an daoine bàs,
an do rinn iad bàgh air an rachadh an iargain 's an ciùrradh seachad,
's am fuiricheadh freumh an duilisg luraich an sàs?

Ach ged bheireadh miann an duilisg duine a thaobh car ùine,
tha 'm bradan lainnireach sìnt' fo shàmhchar dorch,
is ma bheir mi an sgobadh sin air an àit sam bì e
bidh maistreadh fairg ann, is cearcaill sìth 'na lorg.

A geo in the sun's shelter

There is peace in the bay tonight, and the tide swings past the headland;
foam on the hidden rock, wave-lapping at the cliff;
the distant wave cries, and the seas go coursing swiftly,
but this sea is at rest, with no boat at harbour.

Where it dug out a quiet pool with the un-ease of days past,
a geo in the sun's shelter, its pebbles unstained,
where the white years of the moon might pass beyond it,
lunatic, unresting, desirelessly seeking a haven.

The salmon left the sea when this quiet bay was made,
seeking the fresh river – if one moved a stone
the quicksilver lightning-flash of wisdom and knowledge
would tear the still crystal waters of the ducks and the scarts.

At a rock here on the shore the women awaited
the return of the small fishing-boats in storm;
often losing treasure of sea and treasure of bosom,
and feeling the red taste of the salmon salt on their lips.

Often standing watching the sea where their share was lost,
and sitting in houses where their kin had died,
did they make a bay that longing and hurting could by-pass,
where the root of the darling dulse could keep its hold?

Though desire for dulse might for a time entice one,
the shining salmon lies in dark repose,
and if I quickly thrust where he lies hidden,
the water, churned, will leave its rings of peace.

Dh'fhairich mi thu le mo chasan

Dh'fhairich mi thu le mo chasan
ann an toiseach an t-samhraidh;
m' inntinn an seo anns a' bhaile
a' strì ri tuigse, 's na brògan a' tighinn eadarainn.
Tha dòigh an leanaibh duilich a thrèigsinn:
e ga shuathadh fhèin ri mhàthair
gus a faigh e fois.
Dh'fhairich mi taobh an ascaoin dhìot 's an taobh caoin
's cha bu mhisde,
dà thaobh an fheòir is dà ghrèim air an eòrna,
riasg is còinneach,
is bhon a tha an saoghal a bh' againn
a' leantainn ruinn chon a' cheum as fhaide
chan fhiach dhomh am poll sin a ghlanadh
tha eadar òrdagan a' bhalaich.
Agus a-nis aig meadhon latha
tha mi dol a-steach gha mo gharadh,
le mo chasan-rùisgte air fàd ri taobh na cagailt.

I got the feel of you with my feet

I got the feel of you with my feet
in early summer;
my mind here in the city
strives to know, but the shoes come between us.
The child's way is difficult to forget:
he rubs himself against his mother
till he finds peace.
I felt the rough side of you and the smooth
and was none the worse of it,
the two sides of the grass and the two grips on the barley,
peat-fibre and moss,
and since the world we knew
follows us as far as we go
I need not wash away that mud
from between the boy's toes.
And now, in middle age,
I am going in to warm myself,
with my bare feet on a peat beside the hearth.

Is dubh a choisich thu latha

Is dubh a choisich thu latha
a' caoidh nan gallan bu bhòidhche,
'na do ghurraban cràbhaidh
ann am fàsach do sheòmair,

le d' aparan geur
suathadh dheur 's sgapadh sòlais:
thog an iolaire 'na spòig
mire 'n ògain bhon chòmhradh.

Is thubhairt thu gur h-e toil Dhè a bh' ann
gun deach am bàta sin air na Biastan,
a' dìochuimhneachadh na chual' thu ás a' chùbainn:
gu robh Abharsair nan iomadh riochd a sàs unnad.

Black you walked through the day

Black you walked through the day
mourning the handsomest youths,
crouching mumbling piety
in the waste of your room,

your bitter apron
wiping tears and routing joy:
the eagle lifted in his talons
the youth's mirth out of the talk.

And you said it was God's will
that that ship went on the Beasts,
forgetting what you had heard from the pulpit:
that the Adversary of many guises was working on you.

The reference is to the *Iolaire* (Eagle) which was wrecked
on the Beasts of Holm, near Stornoway, drowning a large
number of returning servicemen, at the end of the First
World War.

Cisteachan-laighe

Duin' àrd, tana
's fiasag bheag air,
's locair 'na làimh:
gach uair theid mi seachad
air bùth-shaoirsneachd sa' bhaile,
's a thig gu mo chuinnlean fàileadh na min-sàibh,
thig gu mo chuimhne cuimhne an àit ud,
le na cisteachan-laighe,
na h-ùird 's na tairgean,
na sàibh 's na sgeilbean,
is mo sheanair crom,
is sliseag bho shliseag ga locradh
bhon bhòrd thana lom.

Mus robh fhios agam dè bh' ann bàs;
beachd, bloigh fios, boillsgeadh
den dorchadas, fathann den t-sàmhchair.
'S nuair a sheas mi aig uaigh,
là fuar Earraich, cha dainig smuain
thugam air na cisteachan-laighe
a rinn esan do chàch:
's ann a bha mi 'g iarraidh dhachaigh,
far am biodh còmhradh, is tea, is blàths.

Is anns an sgoil eile cuideachd,
san robh saoir na h-inntinn a' locradh,
cha tug mi'n aire do na cisteachan-laighe,
ged a bha iad 'nan suidhe mun cuairt orm;
cha do dh'aithnich mi 'm brèid Beurla,
an lìomh Gallda bha dol air an fhiodh,
cha do leugh mi na facail air a' phràis,
cha do thuig mi gu robh mo chinneadh a' dol bàs.
Gus an dainig gaoth fhuar an Earraich-sa
a locradh a' chridhe;
gus na dh'fhairich mi na tairgean a' dol tromham,
's cha shlànaich tea no còmhradh an cràdh.

Coffins

A tall thin man
with a short beard,
and a plane in his hand:
whenever I pass
a joiner's shop in the city,
and the scent of sawdust comes to my nostrils,
memories return of that place,
with the coffins,
the hammers and nails,
saws and chisels,
and my grandfather, bent,
planing shavings
from a thin, bare plank.

Before I knew what death was;
or had any notion, a glimmering
of the darkness, a whisper of the stillness.
And when I stood at his grave,
on a cold Spring day, not a thought
came to me of the coffins
he made for others:
I merely wanted home
where there would be talk, and tea, and warmth.

And in the other school also,
where the joiners of the mind were planing,
I never noticed the coffins,
though they were sitting all round me;
I did not recognise the English braid,
the Lowland varnish being applied to the wood,
I did not read the words on the brass,
I did not understand that my race was dying.
Until the cold wind of this Spring came
to plane the heart;
until I felt the nails piercing me,
and neither tea nor talk will heal the pain.

Clann-nighean an sgadain

An gàire mar chraiteachan salainn
ga fhroiseadh bho 'm beul,
an sàl 's am picil air an teanga,
's na miaran cruinne, goirid a dheanadh giullachd,
no a thogadh leanabh gu socair, cuimir,
seasgair, fallain,
gun mhearachd,
's na sùilean cho domhainn ri fèath.

B' e bun-os-cionn na h-eachdraidh a dh'fhàg iad
'nan tràillean aig ciùrairean cutach,
thall 's a-bhos air Galldachd 's an Sasainn.
Bu shaillte an duais a thàrr iad
ás na mìltean bharaillean ud,
gaoth na mara geur air an craiceann,
is eallach a' bhochdainn 'nan ciste,
is mara b' e an gàire
shaoileadh tu gu robh an teud briste.

Ach bha craiteachan uaille air an cridhe,
ga chumail fallain,
is bheireadh cutag an teanga
slisinn á fanaid nan Gall –
agus bha obair rompa fhathast
nuair gheibheadh iad dhachaigh,
ged nach biodh maoin ac':
air oidhche robach gheamhraidh,
ma bha siud an dàn dhaibh,
dheanadh iad daoine.

The herring girls

Their laughter like a sprinkling of salt
showered from their lips,
brine and pickle on their tongues,
and the stubby short fingers that could handle fish,
or lift a child gently, neatly,
safely, wholesomely,
unerringly,
and the eyes that were as deep as a calm.

The topsy-turvy of history had made them
slaves to short-arsed curers,
here and there in the Lowlands, in England.
Salt the reward they won
from those thousands of barrels,
the sea-wind sharp on their skins,
and the burden of poverty in their kists,
and were it not for their laughter
you might think the harp-string was broken.

But there was a sprinkling of pride on their hearts,
keeping them sound,
and their tongues' gutting-knife
would tear a strip from the Lowlanders' mockery –
and there was work awaiting them
when they got home,
though they had no wealth:
on a wild winter's night,
if that were their lot,
they would make men.

Am bodach-ròcais

An oidhch' ud
thàinig am bodach-ròcais dhan taigh-chèilidh:
fear caol àrd dubh
is aodach dubh air.
Shuidh e air an t-sèis
is thuit na cairtean ás ar làmhan.
Bha fear a siud
ag innse sgeulachd air Conall Gulban
is reodh na faclan air a bhilean.
Bha boireannach 'na suidh' air stòl
ag òran, 's thug e'n toradh ás a' cheòl.
Ach cha do dh'fhàg e falamh sinn:
thug e òran nuadh dhuinn,
is sgeulachdan na h-àird an Ear,
is sprùilleach de dh'fheallsanachd Geneva,
is sguab e' n teine á meadhon an làir
's chuir e 'n tùrlach loisgeach nar broillichean.

Aig Tursachan Chalanais

Cha robh toiseach no deireadh air a' chearcall,
cha robh ìochdar no uachdar aig ar smuain,
bha an cruinne-cè balbh a' feitheamh,
gun muir a' slìobadh ri tràigh,
gun feur a' gluasad ri gaoith,
cha robh là ann no oidhche –
is gu sìorraidh cha chaill mi cuimhne
air do chuailean bàn 's do bheul meachair,
no air an aon-dùrachd a shnaoidh sinn
ri chèile an cearcall na tìme,
far nach suath foill ann an tràigh dòchais.

Scarecrow

That night
the scarecrow came into the cèilidh-house:
a tall, thin black-haired man
wearing black clothes.
He sat on the bench
and the cards fell from our hands.
One man
was telling a folktale about Conall Gulban
and the words froze on his lips.
A woman was sitting on a stool,
singing songs, and he took the goodness out of the music.
But he did not leave us empty-handed:
he gave us a new song,
and tales from the Middle East,
and fragments of the philosophy of Geneva,
and he swept the fire from the centre of the floor
and set a searing bonfire in our breasts.

Aig an uinneig

''S thug an dorchadas dhìom-sa Mùirneag.'

Ged nach fhaod mi cianalas
a chur ann an ionad beatha,
is stiallagan de sheann bhruadairean
a chàradh ri uinneig mo thaighe
mar nach biodh saoghal ùr ann,
's a' ghrian a' deàlradh air aodann leanaibh –
gidheadh, tha meadhon na Màigh seo
a' toirt 'nam chuimhne làithean eile,

Mun do thuit a' bhrat, mun do shrac
mi 'n cùmhnant, mun do mhùch
mi 'n t-iarrtas, mun do dh'fhàg
mi beàrn a dh'fhàg beàrn,
mun do sheòl mi air a' *Mhetagàma* bheag
fhurasd ud, gun smuain air Mùirneig,
gun dùil ri ciùrradh, gun dòigh
air tilleadh a-rithist. Gun dòigh.

Teann 's ga bheil an uinneag sin dùinte
thig boladh a-steach oirr' gu cùbhraidh geur:
feur is fallas, is cùbhraidheachd fuilt,
is fàileadh cruaidh iodhan an neòinein
sa' mhadainn, mun dainig an call oirnn,
mun dainig a' bhrat eadarainn,
mun deach an sàl 'na mo shùilean,
mun do dhùin mi 'n aisling.

'S cha tug an dorchadas dhìom fhathast
leus a' chian òir sin, is guirme
na h-òg bhlianna a bh' againn,
is bàinead a' chanaich iodhain
mun do mheirg an t-sian e,
is deirge beul na h-oidhche
mun do dhubh na cuislean,
mun do shàmhaich guth an aoibhneis.

At the window

*'We firmly closed every window there was at
took Muirneag* from my sight.'*

Though I may not put longing
in place of living,
nor arrange shreds of old dreams
against the windows of my house,
as though there were no new world to rec
nor the sun shining on a child's face –
still, this time of mid-May
brings other days to my mind,

Before the curtain fell, before I tore up
the agreement, smothered
the desire, left an empty place
that has made an empty place within me,
before I set sail in that small, easy *Metagam*
with no thought of Muirneag,
no expectation of hurting, nor way
of returning again. Without hope.

Tightly although that window is closed,
the scent comes in fragrant and sharp:
grass and sweat, and the fragrance of hair,
and the hard pure scent of the daisy,
in the morning, before destruction overtook
before the veil came between us,
before the brine got in my eyes,
before I closed the dream.

And darkness has not taken away from me yet
the light of that far gold, and the greenness
of the young year that we had,
and the whiteness of the pure cotton-grass,
before the wind and rain rusted it,
and the redness of approaching night
before the arteries blackened,
before the voice of exultation became still.

At Callanish Stones

The circle had neither end nor beginning,
our thought had neither start nor finish,
the still universe was waiting,
sea not stroking the land,
grass not moving in wind,
there was no day, no night –
and I shall never forget
your fair hair and tender lips,
or the shared desire that wove us
together in time's circle
where treachery will not touch hope's shore.

An tobar

Tha tobar beag am meadhon a' bhaile
's am feur ga fhalach,
am feur gorm sùghor ga dhlùth thughadh,
fhuair mi brath air bho sheann chaillich,
ach thuirt i, "Tha 'm frith-rathad fo raineach
far am minig a choisich mi le m' chogan,
's tha 'n cogan fhèin air dèabhadh."
Nuair sheall mi 'na h-aodann preasach
chunnaic mi 'n raineach a' fàs mu thobar a sùilean
's ga fhalach bho shireadh 's bho rùintean,
's ga dhùnadh 's ga dhùnadh.

"Cha teid duine an diugh don tobar tha sin,"
thuirt a' chailleach,'"mar a chaidh sinne
nuair a bha sinn òg,
ged tha 'm bùrn ann cho brèagh 's cho geal."
'S nuair sheall mi troimhn raineach 'na sùilean
chunnaic mi lainnir a' bhùirn ud
a nì slàn gach ciùrradh
gu ruig ciùrradh cridhe.

"Is feuch an tadhail thu dhomhsa,"
thuirt a' chailleach,'"ga b' ann le meòirean,
's thoir thugam boinne den uisge chruaidh sin
a bheir rudhadh gu m' ghruaidhean."
Lorg mi an tobar air èiginn
's ged nach b' ise bu mhotha feum air
's ann thuice a thug mi 'n eudail.

Dh'fhaodadh nach eil anns an tobar
ach nì a chunnaic mi 'm bruadar,
oir nuair chaidh mi an diugh ga shireadh
cha d'fhuair mi ach raineach is luachair,
's tha sùilean na caillich dùinte
's tha lì air tighinn air an luathghair.

The well

Right in the village there's a little well
and the grass hides it,
green grass in sap closely thatching it.
I heard of it from an old woman
but she said: "The path is overgrown with bracken
where I often walked with my cogie,
and the cogie itself is warped."
When I looked in her lined face
I saw the bracken growing round the well of her eyes,
and hiding it from seeking and from desires,
and closing it, closing it.

"Nobody goes to that well now,"
said the old woman, "as we once went,
when we were young,
though its water is lovely and white."
And when I looked in her eyes through the bracken
I saw the sparkle of that water
that makes whole every hurt
till the hurt of the heart.

"And will you go there for me,"
said the old woman, "even with a thimble,
and bring me a drop of that hard water
that will bring colour to my cheeks."
I found the well at last,
and though her need was not the greatest
it was to her I brought the treasure.

It may be that the well
is something I saw in a dream,
for today when I went to seek it
I found only bracken and rushes,
and the old woman's eyes are closed
and a film has come over their merriment.

An Ceistear

"An dùil,"
ars an duine caomh rium,
"am bi sinn còmhla ri chèile
anns an t-sìorraidheachd?"
Ceist fhuar ann am meadhon an t-samhraidh.
Bha i na b' fhaisg aire-san,
's bha e 'n geall oirr';
bha an t-àit ud
dha mar dhachaigh nach do dh'fhidir e
bho thùs òige,
tlàth ann an suaineadh na cuimhne,
seasgair ann am brù mac-meanmain,
ach mireanach mar adhar earraich;
bha e coiseachd thuice
troimh mhàgh sheargte,
troimhn an fhàsach
às an èireadh na beanntan,
's air chùl fàire
bha tobar is teinntean.
Bha e 'g iarraidh
gu lorgadh a chàirdean an t-slighe,
's gu ruigeadh iad air a socair fhèin;
cha robh e cur cabhaig orra,
chan eil dùil no cabhag anns an t-sìorraidheachd.

The Catechist

"Do you expect,"
said the kindly man to me,
"we shall be together
in eternity?"
A cold question in midsummer.
It was closer to him
and he longed for it;
that place
was to him like a home he had not known
since early youth,
warm in the folds of memory,
sheltered in the imagination's womb,
but merry like a Spring night-sky;
he was walking towards it
over a withered plain,
through the wilderness
out of which the mountains would rise,
and beyond the horizon
there was a well, and a hearth.
He wanted
his friends to find the way,
and they would arrive in their own good time;
he did not hustle them,
there is neither expectation nor hustling in eternity.

Srath Nabhair

Anns an adhar dhubh-ghorm ud,
àirde na sìorraidheachd os ar cionn,
bha rionnag a' priobadh ruinn
's i freagairt mireadh an teine
ann an cabair taigh m' athar
a' bhliadhna thugh sinn an taigh le bleideagan sneachda.

Agus siud a' bhliadhna cuideachd
a shlaod iad a' chailleach don t-sitig,
a shealltainn cho eòlach 's a bha iad air an Fhìrinn,
oir bha nid aig eunlaith an adhair
(agus cròthan aig na caoraich)
ged nach robh àit aice-se anns an cuireadh i a ceann fòidhpe.

A Shrath Nabhair 's a Shrath Chill Donnain,
is beag an t-iongnadh ged a chinneadh am fraoch àlainn oirbh,
a' falach nan lotan a dh'fhàg Pàdraig Sellar 's a sheòrsa,
mar a chunnaic mi uair is uair boireannach cràbhaidh
a dh'fhiosraich dòrainn an t-saoghail-sa
is sìth Dhè 'na sùilean.

Strathnaver

In that blue-black sky,
as high above us as eternity,
a star was winking at us,
answering the leaping flames of fire
in the rafters of my father's house,
that year we thatched the house with snowflakes.

And that too was the year
they hauled the old woman out on to the dung-heap,
to demonstrate how knowledgeable they were in Scripture,
for the birds of the air had nests
(and the sheep had folds)
though she had no place in which to lay down her head.

O Strathnaver and Strath of Kildonan,
it is little wonder that the heather should bloom on your slopes,
hiding the wounds that Patrick Sellar, and such as he, made,
just as time and time again I have seen a pious woman
who has suffered the sorrow of this world,
with the peace of God shining from her eyes.

Mu chrìochan Hòil (earrainn)

. . .

Air madainn Earraich bhiodh a' chaora throm
a' sgaoileadh blàths a bodhaig air an fhonn,
an sneachd a' teicheadh bhuaipe, mar le iochd
don chreutair mheirbh bha gluasad staigh 'na brù,
bodaich is balaich bheaga air a tòir,
sgealbadh bhuntàt' 's a' cur nam mìr 'na beul;
am posta, 's blàth na gaoithe air a ghruaidh,
toirt bràighe air a' chnoc, 's ar sùil ri theachd;
na craobhan, air an lomnochd, nochdadh blàth
an t-snodhaich ann an lìomh nan geug;
am muir, le dath an luaisgein air a gruaidh,
no dath bu duirch na sin, mar gum biodh ciont
nam pronnaidhean 's nam bàthaidhean 'na sùil,
's na creagan liatha tarcaiseach le gàir
a' cur a neart gu neoni leis gach tonn;
na h-eich a' strì ri leathad, 's air an cùl
an treabhaiche, le fèithean cruaidhe teann,
's an fhaoileag, geal ri aghaidh ùir an fhuinn,
mar fhiosaiche an fhoghair bha ri teachd.

Air latha Samhraidh bhiodh ar saoghal cruinn,
gun ghuth air cur no buain, gun cheist air dè
a dh'fhalbh no thigeadh; grian a' sruthadh soills
's na fòid ga sùghadh; cat ga bhlianadh fhèin
far am bu teotha 'chlach; na h-uain ri leum
gun eòlas air an t-sneachd; gaoth fhionnar mhìn
o Ghàrradh Eden trusadh cuimhne fhlùr –
O, fad 's gam mair an latha cha tig crìoch
air guirm' nan neòil is greadhnachas nan uair.

In the vicinity of Hòl (extract)

. . .

On a Spring morning the pregnant sheep
diffused her body-warmth over the ground,
snow retreating from her, showing mercy
to the weakly creature that stirred in her womb,
old men and little boys looking for her,
slicing potatoes and feeding her the pieces;
the post, with weatherbeaten cheeks,
skirting the hill, as we watched for him;
the trees, bare as they were, showing the bloom
of sap in the glisten of their twigs;
the sea, a restless colour on its face,
or a darker hue than that, the guilt
of maulings and of drownings in its eye,
and the grey haughty rocks, laughingly
turning its strength to nothing, with each wave;
horses straining against the brae, behind them
the ploughman, with hard taut sinews,
and the seagull, white against the black soil,
prophesying the coming autumn.

On a Summer day our world was whole,
no thought of sowing, reaping, nor query
of what was gone or was to come; sun shedding light
and turf soaking it in; a cat basking
on the hottest stone; lambs leaping
with no knowledge of snow; a soft fresh breeze
from Eden gathering memories of flowers –
O long as the day is there is no end
to blue skies and hours of joy.

Hòl is the name of a small hill just behind the Bayble
Schoolhouse, Lewis.

'S air feasgar Foghair bhiodh an speal gun sgìos
a' tional bàrr na blianna air a bil;
na balaich, a' cur sùil am fearachas,
gu dian a' ceangal sguab, 's an asbhuain ùr
ga saltairt fo am bròig, 's le dìcheall bhuan
a' deanamh adagan nach maireadh oidhch;
neo a' falach-fead a-measg nan cruachan coirc
le cridhe mear an anmoich, 's gaoth on chuan
slìobadh an sliasaid is an druim le gaoir;
mar dhath an lìonaidh tighinn air a' chuan
bha dath a' chrìonaidh tighinn air an fhraoch,
fàsach an abachaidh a' tional neart
a chuireadh e ri freumhan geala 'n fhàis;
socair na h-asaid air gach fonn is sliabh,
is gàir na mnatha-glùine air gach cnoc.
Eathar 'na siubhal air muir dorcha, trom,
muir m' eilein, muir mo bhaile, raon an èisg,
'g iarraidh a thadhal is a threabhadh fòs;
fir-chlis na mara, 'n caile-bianan grad,
lasadh mar mhire ann an sùilean òigh'.

Air oidhche Gheamhraidh leigt' an ceòl ma sgaoil:
bhiodh faram air an drochaid, danns gu dian
ri ceòl *melodeon*, eubh is gàir mu seach
is sgiamhail nìonag; bainnsean 's ruith-na-h-oidhch.
Tha leus na gealaich fhathast 'na mo shùil,
is fead na gaoithe daonnan ri mo chluais,
is ionndrain ga mo bhuaireadh air gach stràid
air geamhradh 's caplaid bheò a' chinne-daonn.
Ri àm an reothaidh cha robh fois no sgìos
air lorg na deighe, 's nuair a thigeadh sneachd
bha 'n saoghal ùr, is dh'fheumaist dhol air fheadh.
Bu mhath an làmp' bhith laist sa' mhadainn mhoich,

In the Autumn evening the tireless scythe
gathered the year's produce on its blade;
boys, eager to show their manliness,
busily tying sheaves, the fresh stubble
being trampled underfoot, earnestly
making stooks that would not last a night;
or playing hide-and-seek among the stacks
with hearts gay in the twilight, wind from the sea
stroking their thighs and backs, raising gooseflesh;
like colour of filling tide upon the sea
the colour of withering spread on the heather,
wilderness of ripening gathering strength
to put to the white roots of growth;
relief of childbirth in each field and slope,
cry of the midwife on every hill.
A boat coursing on dark heavy seas,
my island's, my village's, the fish field
that needs to be visited and ploughed;
the sea's northern lights, sudden phosphor gleam,
glowing like merriment in a maiden's eyes.

On Winter nights music would be unleashed:
a hubbub on the bridge, eager dancing
to melodeon music, call and laugh in turn
and girls squealing; weddings and night-courtship.
The moon's light stays in my eye still,
the wind's whistle always at my ear,
and on each street I miss humanity's
winter and living bustle.
In freezing weather one never tired
seeking out ice, and when the snow came
the world was new and must be visited.
A lamp lit in early morning was good,

nar suidhe aig tràth-bracaist, is bu mhath
solais a' bhaile deàrrsadh air a' chnoc,
is lanntairean gan lasadh air an oidhch
aig àm na bleoghainn. Is bu mhath an t-àm
san tigeadh sìneadh air an fheasgar fhann,
's ar sùil ri tuilleadh cleasachd air a' bhlàr.
Bha 'm fonn 'na laighe rùisgte fo ar sùil,
gach lagan 's leathad coisrigte don àm
a dh'fhalbh 's don àm a thigeadh,
lom, mar chaidh a chruthachadh air tùs,
is lom, mar chìteadh e air là na h-as-eirigh,
gun chòmhdach ach a' chuimhne, caoin le caoin
an eòlais ged bha choslas aognaidh fuar.
Nuair thigeadh srannraich gaoithe thar a' chnuic
dh'fhàsadh an talamh cruaidh 's an cridhe mear,
's rachadh an t-anmoch mar am peilear teann
san fheòil a dh'altruim fàs is searg nan ràith.

Bha bhlianna aig a ceann, 's bha 'n ath-tè ùr;
ùr mar a naoidhean dh'fhosglas sùil, 's nach fhaic,
solas a' strì ri duirche ghlaist na gèig,
is neart am broinn na gucaig sgaoileadh bhann;
cnead aig an fhiacail briseadh troimh an fheòil,
faochadh a' chadail, eubh sa' mheadhon-oidhch:
na ballachan a' dlùthadh, cuan a' leum
air fear a chaill a ghrèim air stalla –
's an sin, na h-eòin a' ceilearadh san adhar ghorm,
's an coileach gairm air tom, le òrdugh teann
ag iarraidh biadh na maidne dh' a chuid chearc.
Bha 'n oidhche aig a ceann, 's bha 'n latha ùr.

as we sat at breakfast, it was fine
to see the village lights shining on the hill,
and lanterns lit in the evening
at milking time. And we enjoyed
when the wan evening began to grow lighter,
expectant of longer play out in the open.
The land lay bared under our eyes,
each brae and hollow consecrated
both to past and future,
bare as it had been first of all created,
and bare as it would be at the resurrection,
clothed only in the memory, ripe
with knowing's ripeness though it looked cold and forbidding.
When a noisy gust of wind came over the hill
the ground grew hard and the heart merry,
and dusk went like a forceful bullet
into the flesh the seasons' growth and decay had nourished.

The year was at an end, the next one new;
new like a baby opening unseeing eyes,
light striving with the locked murk of the branch,
strength in the bud throwing off bonds;
the tooth's throb breaking through the gum,
sleep's respite, a cry in the night:
walls closing in, sea leaping
at one who had lost his hold on the cliff –
and then, birds singing in a blue sky,
the cock crowing on a mound, a firm order
for morning food to be brought to his hens.
The night was at an end, the day was new.

A' danns'

A' danns' a' dannsa fon a' ghealaich,
a' ghealach fhuar nach fhàg a faileas,
a' ghealach chuireas sinne dhachaigh,
danns' 's a' danns' 's an oidhche fada;
's fhada leam a' ghealach fhuar,
an oidhche bhuairidh is am fallas,
's fhada bhuam an ceòl a ghluais
an crìdh 's a' chluais is mi 'nam bhalach.

Dancing

Dancing, dancing under the moon,
the cold moon that casts no shadow,
the moon that accompanies us home,
the night long and dancing, dancing;
I long for the cold moon,
the tempting night and sweat in the nostrils,
far away is the music that moved
the heart and the ear when I was a boy.

Ma gheibh mi chaoidh a Ghlòir

Ma gheibh mi chaoidh a Ghlòir
(mar nach eil dùil agam)
's ann air sgiathan ceòl nan salm;
chuala mi 'n diugh, 'nam fhàsach,
preseantair Leòdhasach air an rèidio,
's cha do dh'fhairich mi teas na gainmhich fo mo chasan:
bha riasg fionnar na mòintich fo mo bhonnan,
caora ag ionaltradh ann am poll,
's an oiteag a' gluasad thar a' chanaich.
Tha mi làn chreidsinn
gur h-e Leòdhasach a bhios anns an Naomh Peadair
ma liùgas mi steach air geata.

If I ever make it to Heaven

If I ever make it to Heaven
(not that I expect to)
it will be on the wings of psalm music;
today I heard, in my desert,
a Lewis precentor on the radio,
and I no longer felt the heat of the sand underfoot:
the exhilarating fibre of the moor was under my soles,
a sheep grazing in a bog,
and a light breeze stirring the cotton-grass.
I quite believe
that St. Peter will turn out to be a Lewisman
if I do sneak in at the Gate.

House with trees, Lewis

POEMS BY IAIN CRICHTON SMITH

A' dol dhachaigh

A-màireach thèid mi dhachaigh do m' eilean
a' fiachainn ri saoghal a chur an dìochuimhn'.
Togaidh mi dòrn de fhearann 'nam làmhan
no suidhidh mi air tulach inntinn
a' coimhead "a' bhuachaill aig an sprèidh".

Dìridh (tha mi smaointinn) smeòrach.
Eiridh camhanaich no dhà.
Bidh bàt' 'na laighe ann an deàrrsadh
na grèin iarail: 's bùrn a' ruith
troimh shaoghal shamhlaidhean mo thùir.

Ach bidh mi smaointinn (dh'aindeoin sin)
air an teine mhòr th' air cùl ar smuain,
Nagasàki 's Hiroshìma,
is cluinnidh mi ann an rùm leam fhin
taibhs no dhà a' sìor-ghluasad,

taibhs gach mearachd, taibhs gach cionta,
taibhs gach uair a ghabh mi seachad
air fear leònt' air rathad clachach,
taibhs an neonitheachd a' sgrùdadh
mo sheòmar balbh le aodann cèin,

gu 'm bi an t-eilean mar an àirc
'g èirigh 's a' laighe air cuan mòr
's gun fhios an till an calman tuilleadh
's daoine a' bruidhinn 's a' bruidhinn ri chèile
's bogha-froise maitheanais 'nan deuran.

Going home

Tomorrow I shall go home to my island
trying to put a world into forgetfulness.
I will lift a fistful of its earth in my hands
or I will sit on a hillock of the mind
watching "the shepherd with his sheep".

There will arise (I presume) a thrush.
A dawn or two will break.
There will be a boat lying in the glitter
of the western sun: and water running
through the world of similes of my intelligence.

But I will be thinking (in spite of that)
of the great fire at the back of our thoughts,
Nagasaki and Hiroshima,
and I will hear in a room by myself
a ghost or two ceaselessly moving,

the ghost of each error, the ghost of each guilt,
the ghost of each time I walked past
a wounded man on a stony road,
the ghost of nothingness scrutinising
my dumb room with distant face,

till the island becomes an ark
rising and falling on a great sea
and I not knowing whether the dove will return
and men talking and talking to each other
and the rainbow of forgiveness in their tears.

Tha thu air aigeann m' inntinn

Gun fhios dhomh tha thu air aigeann m' inntinn
mar fhear-tadhail grunnd na mara
le chlogaid 's a dhà shùil mhòir
's chan aithne dhomh ceart d' fhiamh no do dhòigh
an dèidh còig bliadhna shiantan
tìme dòrtadh eadar mise 's tù:

beanntan bùirn gun ainm a' dòrtadh
eadar mise gad shlaodadh air bòrd
's d' fhiamh 's do dhòighean 'nam làmhan fann.
Chaidh thu air chall
am measg lusan dìomhair a' ghrunna
anns an leth-sholas uaine gun ghràdh,

's chan èirich thu chaoidh air bhàrr cuain
a chaoidh 's mo làmhan a' slaodadh gun sgur
's chan aithne dhomh do shlighe idir,
thus' ann an leth-sholas do shuain
a' tathaich aigeann na mara gun tàmh
's mise slaodadh 's a' slaodadh air uachdar cuain.

You are at the bottom of my mind

Without my knowing it you are at the bottom of my mind
like a visitor to the bottom of the sea
with his helmet and his two large eyes
and I do not rightly know your appearance or your manner
after five years of showers
of time pouring between me and you:

nameless mountains of water pouring
between me hauling you on board
and your appearance and manner in my weak hands.
You went astray
among the mysterious plants of the sea-bed
in the green half-light without love,

and you will never rise to the surface
though my hands are hauling ceaselessly
and I do not know your way at all,
you in the half-light of your sleep
haunting the bed of the sea without ceasing
and I hauling and hauling on the surface.

Iolaire

On New Year's Eve 1918 a ship called the Iolaire *left Kyle
of Lochalsh to bring three hundred men home to Lewis
after the war was over. On New Year's morning 1919 the
ship went on the rocks as a result of a navigational error
at the Beasts of Holm, a short distance from Stornoway,
the main town on the island. About two hundred sailors
were drowned. In the following poem I imagine an elder
of the church speaking as he is confronted with this
mind-breaking event.*

The green washed over them. I saw them when
the New Year brought them home. It was a day
that orbed the horizon with an enigma.
It seemed that there were masts. It seemed that men
buzzed in the water round them. It seemed that fire
shone in the water which was thin and white
unravelling towards the shore. It seemed that I
touched my fixed hat which seemed to float and then
the sun illumined fish with naval caps,
names of the vanished ships. In sloppy waves,
in the fat of water, they came floating home
bruising against their island. It is true,
a minor error can inflict this death.
That star is not responsible. It shone
over the puffy blouse, the flapping blue
trousers, the black boots. The seagull swam
bonded to the water. Why not man?
The lights were lit last night, the tables creaked
with hoarded food. They willed the ship to port
in the New Year which would erase the old,
its errant voices, its unpractised tones.

Have we done ill, I ask, my fixed body
a simulacrum of the transient waste,
for everything was mobile, plants that swayed,
the keeling ship exploding and the splayed
cold insect bodies. I have seen your church
solid. This is not. The water pours
into the parting timbers where I ache
above the globular eyes. The slack heads turn
ringing the horizon without sound,
with mortal bells, a strange exuberant flower
unknown to our dry churchyards. I look up.
The sky begins to brighten as before,
remorseless amber, and the bruised blue grows
at the erupting edges. I have known you, God,
not as the playful one but as the black
thunderer from hills. I kneel
and touch this dumb blond head. My hand is scorched.
Its human quality confuses me.
I have not felt such hair so dear before
nor seen such real eyes. I kneel from you.
This water soaks me. I am running with
its tart sharp joy. I am floating here
in my black uniform. I am embraced
by these green ignorant waters. I am calm.

Na h-eilthirich

A liuthad soitheach a dh'fhàg ar dùthaich
le sgiathan geala a' toirt Chanada orra.
Tha iad mar neapaigearan 'nar cuimhne
's an sàl mar dheòirean,
's anns na croinn aca seòladairean a' seinn
mar eòin air gheugan.
Muir a' Mhàigh ud, gu gorm a' ruith,
gealach air an oidhche, grian air an latha,
ach a' ghealach mar mheas buidhe,
mar thruinnsear air balla,
ris an tog iad an làmhan,
no mar mhagnet airgeadach
le gathan goirte
a' sruthadh don chridhe.

The exiles

The many ships that left our country
with white wings for Canada.
They are like handkerchiefs in our memories
and the brine like tears
and in their masts sailors singing
like birds on branches.
That sea of May, running in such blue,
a moon at night, a sun at daytime,
and the moon like a yellow fruit,
like a plate on a wall,
to which they raise their hands,
like a silver magnet
with piercing rays
streaming into the heart.

Do mo mhàthair

Bha thus' a' sgoltadh sgadain
ann a Yarmouth fad' air falbh
's a' ghrian shaillt sa mhadainn
ag èirigh às a' chuan
's an fhuil air oir do sgine
's an salainn ud cho garbh
's gun thachd e thu o bhruidhinn
's gu robh do bhilean searbh.

Bha mis' an Obar-Dheadhain
a' deoghal cùrsan ùr',
mo Ghàidhlig ann an leabhar
's mo Laideann aig an stiùir,
'nam shuidh' an siud air cathair
's mo chofaidh ri mo thaobh
is duilleagan a' crathadh
siùil na sgoilearachd 's mo thùir.

Tha cionta ga mo lèireadh
mar a dh'èirich 's mar a tha.
Cha bu chaomh leam a bhith 'g èirigh
ann an doilleireachd an là,
bhith a' sgoltadh 's a bhith reubadh
iasg na maidne air an tràigh
's am muir borb ud a bhith beucadh
sìos mo mhiotagan gun tàmh.

Ged a nì mi sin 'nam bhàrdachd,
's e m' fhuil fhìn a th' air mo làimh,
's gach aon sgadan thug an làn dhomh
a' plosgartaich gu 'n dèan mi dàn,
's an àite cùbair tha mo chànan
cruaidh is teann orm a ghnàth
is an salainn garbh air m' fhàinne
a' toirt beòthalachd don bhàs.

To my mother

You were gutting herring
in distant Yarmouth
and the salt sun in the morning
rising out of the sea,
the blood on the edge of your knife,
and that salt so coarse
that it stopped you from speaking
and made your lips bitter.

I was in Aberdeen
sucking new courses,
my Gaelic in a book
and my Latin at the tiller,
sitting there on a chair
with my coffee beside me
and leaves shaking the sails
of scholarship and my intelligence.

Guilt is tormenting me
because of what happened and how things are.
I would not like to be getting up
in the darkness of the day
gutting and tearing
the fish of the morning on the shore
and that savage sea to be roaring
down my gloves without cease.

Though I do that in my poetry
it is my own blood that is on my hands,
and every herring that the high tide gave me
palpitating till I make a song,
and instead of a cooper my language
always hard and strict on me,
and the coarse salt on my ring
bringing animation to death.

Am faigh a' Ghàidhlig bàs? (earrainnean)

2

Sanasan-reice ann an neon
a' dol thuige 's a' dol as,
'Am faigh a' . . . am faigh a',
   am faigh a' Ghàidhlig
     am faigh a' . . .
     am faigh a' Ghàidhlig
     . . . bàs?'

3

Tha facail ag èirigh às an dùthaich.
Tha iad mun cuairt oirnn.
Anns gach mìos anns a' bhliadhna
tha sinn air ar cuartachadh le facail.

Tha fhaclair fhèin aig an earrach,
na duilleagan a' tionndadh
ann an gaoth bhiorach a' Mhàirt.
Tha i fosgladh nam bùithtean.

Tha fhaclair fhèin aig an fhoghar,
na duilleagan donna
'nan laighe air aigeann na linne
'nan cadal 'son seuson.

Tha fhaclair fhèin aig a' gheamhradh,
tha na facail 'nan cathadh
a' togail an turraid ud, Bàbel.
Tha a ghràmar mar shneachd.

Shall Gaelic die? (extracts)

2
Advertisements in neon,
lighting and going out,
'shall it . . . shall it . . .
    Shall Gaelic . . .
        shall it . . .
        shall Gaelic
        . . . die?'

3
Words rise out of the country.
They are around us.
In every month in the year
we are surrounded by words.

Spring has its own dictionary,
its leaves are turning
in the sharp wind of March,
which opens the shops.

Autumn has its own dictionary,
the brown leaves
lying on the bottom of the loch,
asleep for a season.

Winter has its own dictionary,
the words are a blizzard
building a tower of Babel.
Its grammar is like snow.

Eadar na facail tha an cat-fiadhaich
a' toirt sùil gheur tarsainn
air talamh nach buin do dhuine,
urchraichean a' Mhic-meanmna.

4
Thog iad taigh
le clachan.
Chuir iad uinneagan anns an taigh
is dorsan.
Lìon iad na rumannan le furniture
's le feusagan nam fòghnan.

Sheall iad a-mach às an taigh
air saoghal Gàidhealach.
Na dìtheanan, na gleanntan,
Glaschu fad' air falbh
'na theine.

Thog iad barometer eachdraidh.

Oirleach an dèidh òirlich, dh'fhuiling iad
gathan an fhulangais.

Thàinig coigrich a-steach don taigh, 's dh'fhalbh iad.

Ach, a-nis,
cò tha sealltainn a-mach
le aodann atharraicht?

Dè tha e coimhead?

Dè th' aige 'na làimh?

Gad de fhacail ùra.

Between the words the wild-cat
looks sharply across
a No-Man's-Land,
artillery of the Imagination.

4
They built a house
with stones.
They put windows in the house,
and doors.
They filled the room with furniture
and the beards of thistles.

They looked out of the house
on a Highland world,
the flowers, the glens,
distant Glasgow
on fire.

They built a barometer of history.

Inch after inch, they suffered
the stings of suffering.

Strangers entered the house, and they left.

But now,
who is looking out
with an altered gaze?

What does he see?

What has he got in his hand?

A string of new words.

5

Am fear a chailleas a chànan,
caillidh e a shaoghal.
An Gàidheal a chailleas a chànan,
caillidh e an saoghal.

An soitheach a chailleas na planaidean,
caillidh i an saoghal.

Ann an saoghal orange,
ciamar a dh'aithnicheadh tu orange?
Ann an saoghal gun olc,
ciamar a dh'aithnicheadh tu am math?

Tha Wittgenstein am meadhon a shaoghail.
Tha e mar dhamhan-allaidh.
Tha na cuileagan a' tighinn thuige.
"Cuan" is "coille" a' dìreadh.

Nuair a thèid Wittgenstein às,
thèid a shaoghal às.

Tha am fòghnan a' lùbadh chun an làir.

Tha an talamh sgìth dheth.

5

He who loses his language
loses his world.
The Highlander who loses his language
loses his world.

The space ship that goes astray among planets
loses the world.

In an orange world
how would you know orange?
In a world without evil
how would you know good?

Wittgenstein is in the middle of his world.
He is like a spider.
The flies come to him.
'Cuan' and 'coill' rising.*

When Wittgenstein dies,
his world dies.

The thistle bends to the earth.

The earth is tired of it.

---

* *Cuan* means 'sea' and *coill* means 'wood'.

Leòdhas

Bhon Chuimhneachan Cogaidh
chì sinn Leòdhas air fad.
Airson an àite seo bhàsaich iad,
na taighean ùra, fàileadh an fheamainn,
na h-aibhnichean.
Cailleach a' falbh air feadh a fearainn,
a' ghaoth air a' Chuan Siar,
faoileag 'na laighe marbh air rubha lom.
An cuan a' briseadh geal air gainmheach fhada,
flùrain am measg nan clach.
Ministear air sràidean Steòrnabhaigh
air latha fliuch is fuar.
Airson an àite seo bhàsaich iad.
Tha ùrnaighean air claoidh
na daoine aosda tinn.
Tha a' ghaoth a' bualadh air na rubhachan,
cho aonaranach a' seinn,
a' mhòinteach buidhe le na dìtheanan,
na lochan beaga grinn
mar fhàinnichean gorma gus an robh iad uair
a' coiseachd 's iad 'nan clann.

Beart na gaoithe air na rubhachan
gu buan a' dèanamh srann.

Lewis

From the War Memorial
we see Lewis entirely.
For this place they died,
the new houses, the smell of seaweed,
the rivers,
an old woman walking about her croft,
the wind on the Atlantic,
a seagull lying dead on a bare headland,
the sea breaking whitely on the long sand,
flowers among the stones,
a minister on a Stornoway street
on a cold wet day.
For this place they died.
Prayers are exhausting
the old sick people.
The wind is beating against the headlands
with its lonely song,
the moor yellow with flowers,
the small elegant lochs
like blue rings, where they used to walk
when they were children.

The loom of the wind on the headlands
with its eternal whine.

Meileòidian an spioraid

E hì o ró, e hì o rì,
danns, danns, air an rathad.
O mheileòidiain an spioraid,
danns, danns aig ceann a' ghàrraidh.

O mheileòidiain an spioraid,
O làmhan fad' às
fann is geal ann an gealach foghair,
O na casan èasgaidh bras.

O mheileòidiain an spioraid,
uaine 's dearg is uaine rithist,
tha taibhsichean aig ceann a' ghàrraidh,
tha ar cuid dheòirean a' sileadh.

Tha ceòl ùr aig ceann ar meòirean.
Danns, danns air an rathad.
O mheileòidiain mo dheòirean,
tha 'n ceòl ùr a' deàrrsadh thairis

gealach abachaidh an eòrna,
gealach òir na h-oidhche fhada,
gealach bhalach, gealach Leòdhais,
gealach bhrògan an ùr-fhasain.

The melodeon of the spirit

E hi o ro, e hi o ri,
dance, dance on the road.
O melodeon of the spirit,
dance, dance at the end of the garden.

O melodeon of the spirit,
O distant hands
faint and white in an autumn moon,
O the active rash feet.

O melodeon of the spirit,
green and red and green again,
there are ghosts at the end of the garden,
our tears are falling.

There is a new music at the tips of our fingers,
dance, dance on the road.
O melodeon of my tears,
the new music is shining over

the ripening moon of the barley,
the golden moon of the long night,
the moon of boys, the moon of Lewis,
the moon of the shoes of the new fashion.

From *A Life*

Lewis 1928-1945

1

'When did you come home? When are you leaving?'
'No, I don't . . . don't think I know . . .'
The moonlit autumn nights of long ago,
the heavy thump of feet at their late dancing.
'We'll sail by the autumn moon to Lewis home.'
'I think I know you . . .' But our faces age,
our knuckles redden and webbed lines engage
eyes that were once so brilliant and blue.
The sharp salt teaches us. These houses, new
and big with grants and loans, replace the old
thatched walls that straggled in a tall lush field.
I lie among the daisies and look up
into a tall blue sky where lost larks chirp.
The sea is blazing with a bitter flame.
'When are you leaving? When did you come home?'
The island is the anvil where was made
the puritanical heart. The daisies foam
out of the summer grass. The rigid dead
sleep by the Bràighe, tomb on separate tomb.

Young girl singing psalm

Just for a moment then as you raised your book –
it must have been the way your glasses looked

above the round red cheeks – as you poured out
the psalm's grim music from a pulsing throat,

that moment, as I say, I saw you stand
thirty years hence, the hymn book in your hand,

a fleshy matron who are now sixteen.
The skin is coarser, you are less serene.

What now is fervour is pure habit then.
To bridge devoted and to thought immune,

a connoisseur of flowers and sales of work,
you cycle through round noons where no sins lurk,

your large pink hat a garden round your head,
the cosy wheel of comfort and of God.

And, as I see you, matron of that day,
I wonder, girl, which is the better way –

in innocent fervour tackling antique verse,
or pink Persephone, innocently coarse.

Do sheana-bhoireannach

Tha thu san eaglais ag èisdeachd
air being mhì-chomhfhurtail ri briathran
fear nach eil ach leth do bhliadhnan.

'S tha mise 'nam shuidhe seo a' sgrìobhadh
na facail chearbach-s': gun fhios 'n e 'n fhìrinn
no bhreug bhòidheach tha 'nam inntinn.

Ach, aon tè tha tighinn air m' inntinn,
thusa 'nad shuidhe air beulaibh cùbainn
'nad aid dhuibh shìmplidh: 'na do chòta
(dubh cuideachd) 's 'na do bhrògan
a choisich iomadh sràid mhòr leat.

Cha b' e sgoilear thu 'na do latha.
('S iomadh madainn a sgoilt thu sgadan
's a bha do làmhan goirt le salainn,
's a' ghaoth gheur air oir do sgine,
's d' òrdagan reòit' le teine.)

Cha chuala tusa mu dheidhinn Dharwin
no Fhreud no Mharx no 'n Iùdhaich eile,
Einstein leis an inntinn ealant':
no ciall a' bhruadair a bhruadraich thu
's thu 'n raoir 'nad rùm 'nad theann-chadal.
Cha chuala tu mar a theicheas na reultan
mar bhan-righinnean ciùin troimh na speuran,
's cha chuala tu mar a shuidheas an leòmhann
le ceann borb aig a' bhòrd leinn.

To an old woman

You are in the church listening,
sitting on an uncomfortable bench
to the words of one who is only half your age.

And I am sitting here writing
these corrupted words, and not knowing whether it is the truth
or the beautiful lie that is in my mind.

But there is one person who comes into my mind,
you sitting in front of a pulpit
in your simple black hat, and in your coat
(black as well) and in your shoes
that have walked many a long street with you.

You were not a scholar in your day.
(Many a morning did you gut herring,
and your hands were sore with salt,
and the keen wind on the edge of your knife,
and your fingers frozen with fire.)

You have never heard of Darwin
or Freud or Marx or that other Jew,
Einstein, with the brilliant mind:
nor do you know the meaning of the dream you dreamed
last night in your room in heavy sleep.
You haven't heard how the stars move away from us
like calm queens through the sky.
And you haven't heard how the lion
with his fierce head sits at the table with us.

Ach suidhidh tu 'n sin air beulaibh cùbainn
's nì thu 'nad aonranachd iomadh ùrnaigh
's ma bheireas am ministear air làimh ort
bithidh toileachas a' lìonadh d' inntinn.

Cuimhnichidh tu air làithean eile,
searmon cho dìreach ris a' pheileir,
samhradh a' dòrtadh timcheall eaglais,
fàinne òir is teisteanas
ròsan a' fosgladh samhraidh
mar ùr-Bhìobull 'na do chuimhne.

'S cuimhnichidh tu air iomadh bàs
is iomadh latha a chaidh fàs,
uaireadair anns na ballachan
a' diogadh do shaoghail gu a cheann.

Gu soirbhich do shaoghal gu math leat
's tu nise air do shlighe dhachaigh
troimh shràidean geal mar inntinn duine
fosgailt' le oir na sgine,
's balaich 'nan seasamh 'nan cuid aimhreit
a' sgrùdadh neonitheachd: 's geur a sheall iad
riutsa falbh, gun armachd, tarsainn
sràid a' losgadh mu do chasan,
gun armachd ach do spiorad còrdail
nach do chuir saoghal riamh an òrdugh
ach a chumas tu, tha mi 'n dòchas,
slàn 'nad neochiontas mar chòta.

But you sit there in front of the pulpit
and in your loneliness you say many a prayer
and if the minister shakes you by the hand
your mind is filled with happiness.

You remember other days,
a sermon direct as a bullet,
a summer pouring around a church,
a gold ring and the testimony
of roses opening summer
like a new Bible in your memory.

And you will remember many a death
and many days which went waste,
a clock in the wall
ticking your world to its end.

May your world prosper
and you on your way home
over the white streets like a man's mind,
open with the edge of the knife,
and boys standing in their quarrelsomeness
studying nothingness: keenly they looked
at you going without armour across
a street burning at your feet,
without armour but your harmonious spirit
that never put a world in order
but which will keep you, I hope,
whole in your innocence like a coat.

Aig Clachan Chalanais

Aig clachan Chalanais an-dè
chuala mi tè ag ràdh ri tèile:
"Seo far na loisg iad clann o shean."
Chan fhaca mi draoidhean anns na reultan
no grian no gùn: ach chunna mi
ball brèagha gorm mar nèamh a' sgàineadh
is clann le craiceann slaodadh riutha
mar a' bhratach sna dh'ìobradh Nagasàki.

At the Stones of Callanish

At the stones of Callanish yesterday
I heard one woman saying to another:
'This is where they burnt the children in early times.'
I did not see druids among the planets
nor sun nor robe: but I saw
a beautiful blue ball like heaven cracking
and children with skin hanging to them
like the flag in which Nagasaki was sacrificed.

Farewell my brother (extract)

My distant brother
with your own casket
of joys and tribulations.

Barer than the mind
is the soil of Lewis.
It is in the keeping of the wind.
It has the sea's resonance,

that constant music
that enchanted cottage
which enhanced our residence,

our hunger for the unknown.
If we could speak again
would we know better?

I offer this bouquet
from the oceans of salt,
my distant brother.

I send it across the seas
to the spaciousness of Canada,
my flowering poem,

to let its fragrance
be sweet in your nostrils,
though you are now unable
to converse with me.

My distant brother,
in the shelter of my poem
let you be secret

till we are children again
in the one bed
in the changing weather
of an inquisitive childhood.

The roads separate:
see, I wave to you,
you turn away completely
into your own cloud.

See, I wave to you
you are disappearing forever.
Tears disarm me.

Now you stand like a statue
in the honour of goodness.

My pride and my tears burn me.

Farewell, my brother.

The Tape Runs

The tape runs
bearing its weight of poems
conversations
echoes of past rhymes.

Sometimes I think that time
is odder
than any order
for to gain one future
is to lose another

Calmly the tape runs
The fruit of dead voices
composes
itself on the brown wheels.

They return to us
over and over
in this calm weather
of continuous hum

Dear dead voices
dear dignified ones
I see your bones
in this green focus

narrowing widening
the grass of your burying
small set green window
pulsing with a whole life.

From 'Taynuilt 1982'

16

There is no island.
The sea unites us.
The salt is in our mouth.

I have heard the drowned sing
when the moonlight
casts a road across the waters,
fine and luminous,
and each house sways
in its autumn light.

'The moon that takes us home to Lewis'
to the dancing
to the phantoms of evening
to the charmed wells.

The island, as our poet said,
is an iceberg.
We bear it with us,
our flawed jewel.

As the sun sets
over the mountains
I see the homeless ones
forever rowing.
Their peasant hats mushroom,
like foundering bouquets.

The wakes
are for everyone
and the large sun
glints on the excised names
of the exiles.

'No ebb tide ever came
without a full tide after it' –
precious ones
whose flesh is my own,

and who arise each day
to a new desert.

The island, my vase, knows you.
Your inscribed faces
burn out of the brine:
this is the sharp wine
that educates us.

As we change
so the island changes,
we are not estranged
by the salt billows.

'There is no ebb tide
without a full tide after it.'
The tall white bride
accepts the fresh waters.

Derick Thomson and Iain Crichton Smith in conversation,
being recorded by Julian May

POETS IN CONVERSATION

T HE EXTRACTS following are taken from two radio programmes where one or both poets are talking about their lives and island culture, and are organised by subject. The initials of each poet identify the speaker alongside the word 'Island' or 'Bayble' to signify the radio programme referred to.

The Island Is Always With You. BBC Radio 3 Feature marking the sixtieth birthday of Iain Crichton Smith (1988). Broadcast simultaneously on Radio 3 and Radio Scotland. Selected for *Pick of the Week*.

Described by *Scotland on Sunday* as 'one of the outstanding radio programmes of the year.'

Producer: Stewart Conn

Research, interview and editing: Andrew Mitchell

Extracts identified: (ICS Island)

How Many Miles From Bayble? BBC Radio 4 Kaleidoscope Feature, which took both poets back to Lewis (1995).

Producer: Julian May

Research and interview: Andrew Mitchell

Extracts identified: (ICS Bayble) or (DT Bayble)

THE IMPORTANCE OF THE ISLAND

WHAT LEWIS MEANT TO HIM (ICS Island)

Returning to Lewis is returning to a special way of life
and to a special language, Gaelic. Also, I suppose to a
certain extent, to a special kind of religion.

THE ISLAND OF LEWIS AND POETRY (ICS Island)

It's a very bleak island. There are more trees now than when
I was growing up. It's very bare, very windswept. I've always

thought of my own poetry as having that kind of bareness.

THE SOUND OF THE SEA (ICS Island)

Of course, it being an island, you're conscious all the time of the sound of the sea around you. This is something that I miss, staying where I do in Taynuilt. In some deep sense I miss the sound of the sea.

ISLAND LIFE
IMPORTANT PEOPLE IN VILLAGE SOCIETY (ICS Island)

The two main people who would have had fundamental standing in the society would have been the headmaster and teachers in the school . . . and also, of course, the minister.

SKILLS WITHIN THE VILLAGE (ICS Island)

A lot of these people were good at different kinds of jobs. They were crofters and also fishermen. One thing that used to astonish me was the way they built their own houses, which I thought was quite extraordinary, many having no previous training in masonry or anything like that.

PEAT CUTTING AND SELF-SUFFICIENCY (DT Bayble)

Everybody had their own designated peat banks, which they cut, and they did this in a communal way. They were self-sufficient and didn't have to rely on cash. There was very little cash circulating in the community at that time.

ROAD DANCES (DT Bayble)

One of the great entertainments they had was what was called *danns an rathaid*, dancing on the road. In Bayble a favourite location for this was an old wooden bridge. It had a wooden base, so it was easier to dance on than a gravel road; it had no sides, so you had to be a little careful you didn't topple over the edge . . . We're on the bridge now, but the road has a tarmac top now and concrete sides, so you can't fall off it easily.

AUTUMN DANCES (ICS Island)

I remember on autumn nights especially, at the end of the

road they used to have dances and they played the melodeon . . . something almost trance-like about them. I remember standing at our own house and this very red autumn moon in the sky and hearing the dancing at the end of the road. And it has always remained in my memory as something of extraordinary significance, a perfectly beautiful autumn evening.

ISLAND COMMUNITY (ICS Island)

I suppose a community has two aspects to it. It provides you with a certain kind of warmth and on the other hand it makes you feel slightly claustrophobic, because you always feel you're under the gaze of the other people in the community.

FIRST LANGUAGE
FIRST LANGUAGE (DT Bayble)

I had English for my first language and became bilingual from the age of five or so, but there was a curious situation within the family. Father was quite a prominent Gaelic activist, a writer himself, a writer of prose and poetry and editor. My mother, on the other hand, was extremely interested in Gaelic poetry and song. She virtually sang all day about her work. So, as the years went on, I tended to speak Gaelic mainly with my mother and English mainly with my father, but the two of them switched between the two languages continually.

FIRST LANGUAGE (ICS Island)

Before I went to school we were speaking Gaelic in the house and in the village, and then at the age of five I went to school and learned English and then all my other subjects in English. I can't actually remember how all this happened. We spoke Gaelic in the playground and then when we went back into school we spoke English.

LANGUAGE AND CULTURE IN CHILDHOOD

TENSIONS OF SPEAKING TWO LANGUAGES (ICS Bayble)

I didn't think when I was young in terms of Gaelic as being opposed to English in a nationalistic sense. Gaelic was quite my natural language, so I didn't oppose it to English and consciously say I must keep Gaelic going. At that time Gaelic in the village was just the normal language that you spoke. At the same time there weren't many books, certainly not for children; more now, but in those days not many books at all for children in Gaelic. The children's books that I would be reading would be in English.

FIRST POEM (ICS Island)

When I was eleven years old I composed my first poem. It was not written down. In those days Chamberlain was going to Europe with his umbrella to pacify the Nazis. The Nazis were very different kinds of people who did not know about cricket and so on. I woke up this morning in 1939 and I started reciting, quite spontaneously, this poem in Gaelic about Chamberlain's visits to Europe. This is quite interesting because Gaelic poetry is orally based.

WRITING POETRY (ICS Island)

I started writing poetry, I think, quite young. Mainly because I was ill a lot. I used to suffer from bronchitis and I was off school a lot, so I used to read. I chose to read a lot of poetry.

READING (ICS Island)

I tended to read more English poets than Gaelic poets at that age. In those days they did not have books for children in Gaelic. We didn't have any. I was reading the kind of ordinary English books that anyone would have read, even in England.

LANGUAGE AND CULTURE

LANGUAGE AND SOCIAL FUNCTION (ICS Island)

If I were to go home to Lewis and speak to someone in English from that community, I would be considered aloof, almost aristocratic, as if it were a kind of social thing, as if I was looking down upon them, but if I go back and speak Gaelic to them, that's OK.

Language in a situation like that is not purely linguistic but has a social connotation. Obviously, with a marginal language there is a very, very strong movement to preserve it. You feel this dominating yourself in a way that you feel a certain amount of guilt about it. The fact that I wrote in English as well as Gaelic was difficult as well. I did feel that to write in English was a betrayal of my roots in a sense.

BAYBLE SCHOOL

BAYBLE SCHOOL (DT Bayble)

We're just beside the school at Bayble, where my father was headmaster from 1922 until 1953. I was brought up here (in) my early years and attended the school until the age of thirteen or so . . .

BAYBLE SCHOOL AND BARE FEET (ICS Bayble)

I attended this school as well. In the summer months we used to take off our shoes and run barefoot into school. That's really one of my main memories, running on the grass to school, barefoot under the skylarks.

SHOES AND POVERTY (DT Bayble)

But there were some very poor members of the community; this was where the children, especially boys, came to school all the year round without shoes. I remember boys of my own class walking through the snow with their bare feet.

THE NICOLSON INSTITUTE
BAYBLE SCHOOL AND THE NICOLSON INSTITUTE, STORNOWAY
(DT Bayble)

Bayble School ran through the primary up through the first
three years of the secondary, but not everybody finished
these three years of secondary: it was possible to transfer to
the secondary school in Stornoway, the Nicolson Institute.
When you made that transition, you found yourself in a very
different environment. Perhaps a third of your class would
consist of Stornoway pupils, and the rest of the pupils from
various parts of Lewis and the countryside. Practically all the
rural pupils would be Gaelic-speaking and the great majority
of the Stornoway pupils would be English-speaking, and
some of them, indeed, would have quite contemptuous
attitudes towards Gaelic. For all that, although this was a
traumatic transition in some ways, I remember a new sense
of widening community, because I met people from the West
Side and from Ness, and from Uig and Bernera and from
Lochs, and began to become acquainted with their different
dialects of Gaelic. You lost your original community but you
found a new community; so there were benefits as well as
disadvantages.

WRITTEN AND SPOKEN LANGUAGE AT THE NICOLSON
INSTITUTE AND THE UNIVERSITY OF ABERDEEN (ICS
Bayble)

What happened was that in the playground we very often
spoke English now, rather than Gaelic . . . and Gaelic at
home. So it was quite a complicated existence.

. . . The other thing that happened, of course, was that
you could take Gaelic in the Nicolson as a subject, you
could take Gaelic as you could take French or Latin, and
study it as I did and Derick did too; and then we went off
to Aberdeen University and continued our studies; it
became known as Celtic.

UNIVERSITY OF ABERDEEN
LANGUAGE SPOKEN AT THE UNIVERSITY OF ABERDEEN (DT
    Bayble)
    We got there and found students from previous classes, and
    students from Skye and Harris and various other Gaelic
    localities – Wester Ross. The Gaelic people tended to
    congregate and speak Gaelic practically all the time. Perhaps
    we felt that at Aberdeen we were surrounded by foreigners
    of a kind, and we wanted to assert our own individuality.

EFFECTS OF EDUCATION
EFFECTS OF EDUCATION (ICS Island)
    Anyone who was reasonably bright was educated out of
    the village and eventually out of the island itself . . . The
    brightest elements have to leave the island.

LITERARY COMMITMENT
GAELIC AND NATIONALISM (DT Bayble)
    In my case I had decided by that time fairly firmly to make
    Gaelic studies my main career. That reinforced tendencies
    that had been showing up throughout my secondary
    school, nationalistic tendencies if you like, which I think I
    began to link by my early teens with the language
    question. That probably had a strong effect in the long
    run on my choice of Gaelic as a creative writing language.

COMMITMENT TO WRITING IN GAELIC (DT Bayble)
    I don't think I've ever written an original English poem
    since 1948. I've often written translations of my Gaelic
    poems. Again, there was a strongish political motivation
    behind that, but it wasn't the only one. I think there was
    a strong cultural motivation too. I think I felt at that time
    that whatever I had to say was likely to have stronger
    relevance if it was against a Gaelic background.

READING, POETRY AND WRITING (ICS Bayble)
    The main thing as far as I was concerned was that I was
    looking for writers who were twentieth century writers,
    people like T.S. Eliot and W.H. Auden who were dealing with

twentieth century phenomena, and there weren't a lot of
Gaelic poets at that time who were doing that: Sorley
MacLean had begun to write by that time and I'd read his. I
was writing and I think Derick was writing too, for the
University magazine, *Alma Mater*. I was writing English
poems for *Alma Mater*. After I left University I was writing
short stories, plays and so on in Gaelic; but I think generally
speaking I knew that the main thrust of my work would be
in English. I had always been, I think, more comfortable
writing in English, even though it was my second language.

THE POEM 'FOR MY MOTHER', HIS MOTHER AS A HERRING
GIRL (ICS Island)
There were three of us, three boys. My mother, of course,
was widowed, because my father died when I was two,*
and this meant we were living on a pension of ten
shillings a week,** which even then was not very much.
We could only go to Stornoway once a year and
Stornoway was only seven miles away. This was a red-
letter day in our lives.
Later on when I went to Aberdeen (University) and was
living in this kind of intellectual milieu and talking about
Camus and Sartre and people, I used to think of my
mother at the same age as me, when she would have
been a herring girl, going round the ports of England and
Scotland, gutting herring and getting her hands wounded
with the salt of the herring. In fact I wrote a poem about
that many years afterwards, but I did feel that particular
guilt as well.

THE POEM 'THE HERRING GIRLS', BAYBLE BAY ON SUNDAY
MORNING (DT Bayble)
We're back at Bayble again today. It happens to be
Sunday, so it's quieter than ever. I left Bayble virtually
forty-five years ago, but when it comes to creative writing,

---

* According to Iain's wife Donalda, he may have been three
when his father died. This is based on the age of Iain's
younger brother Kenneth, who was a baby at the time.
** Fifty pence in decimal currency.

I find my thoughts coming back to these scenes, to this
island, to the images that belong to that time. I think,
probably, however long I go on writing, that won't
change. I'm going to read a poem now called 'The
Herring Girls'. It was written in the deep south, round
about Glasgow, looking back towards things in Lewis.

RELIGION AND ISLAND CULTURE
EVANGELICAL RELIGION ON LEWIS (DT Bayble)
The evangelical religion arrived somewhat late in Lewis,
but we have accounts from the third and fourth decades
of the nineteenth century of evangelical ministers
stamping as hard as they could on the local culture.
Ordering people to break their fiddles and break their
pipes and stop singing vain songs.

RELIGION AND LITERATURE (ICS Island)
I found religion on the island quite oppressive, really. It was
very strict. For instance, nothing was ever done on a Sunday.
I found the Sundays enormously long as a child. I have
found that kind of ideology extremely oppressive; and my
attitude is that now I find any kind of ideology hard to
accept. My main feeling about literature is that it should
deal with individual human beings and that any kind of
ideology . . . whether it is ecclesiastical or political . . . is
cutting through a certain section and on both sides of that
section are howling wildernesses that are not being colonised.
I feel an instinctive dislike of any kind of ideology.

FREE CHURCH AND CREATIVITY IN THE ISLAND (ICS
Bayble)
Derick has pointed out one of the important things about
the Free Church in the island: its hostility . . . to the
creative artist. This hasn't declined . . . A cousin of mine
who was Free Church . . . was very ill and we took him
down to Argyll for a few weeks. When we were leaving
the house he said, 'I feel like Joseph going down to
Egypt.' He actually said this!

RELIGION AND SUPERSTITION (DT Bayble)

The lady we were talking to in Keose was recalling how the trees round the house she lives in had been planted by an incoming doctor thirty years ago and he had evidently planted them on a Sunday. Some people in the community told him these trees had very little chance of surviving to adulthood.

Some people couldn't shave; they had to shave on Saturday night ready to go to church on Sunday. Preferably, you didn't even peel the potatoes; you peeled them the previous night. In Bayble young people were allowed to have a walk down to the shore, but not to play football, not to make a noise, anything of that sort.

COCKERELS AND CREELS (ICS Bayble)

The other thing they used to do, which was very strange, was to put the cockerels under a creel, so they wouldn't have sex with the hens.

CEILIDH AND RELIGION

THE CEILIDH HOUSE (ICS Island)

The ceilidh traditionally in the Highlands was that there might be a particular house that people would choose within the village, and then they would go along and would have songs and maybe pipe music and maybe accordion music and so on; and the ceilidh house was a kind of central focus within the community.

THE POEM 'THE SCARECROW' (ICS Island)

Derick Thomson has got a poem in which he talks about the power of Calvinism and the power of religion in relation to that spontaneous ceilidh atmosphere; and he sees in the thatched houses, which were slightly before the time I grew up – the fire was in the centre of the floor and consequently the people would be sitting round the fire in a circle. Later on, Derick Thomson talks about Calvinism replacing this kind of spontaneous community, replacing the fire in the centre of the floor, which was a social fire, with religious hell fire. I thought this was a

very good summing up of what had happened to a great
extent, and the indifference of that kind of religion to a
spontaneous culture.

MARGINAL COMMUNITIES
MARGINAL COMMUNITIES (ICS Island)
> I think that marginal communities like the Highland
> community and the Aboriginal community and possibly
> the Maori community in New Zealand and the Red Indian
> community in America – I think that very often when a
> larger group of people, a more modern civilisation,
> impinges on them, you find . . . these people becoming
> very often alcoholics . . . I think you can find this in the
> Highland community and in the Red Indian community, a
> feeling that another civilisation greater than themselves is
> converging on them, taking over what they had and not
> fully understanding their inner resources. Because, of
> course, the Aboriginal culture was an extraordinarily
> complicated culture: this other civilisation does not really
> care about them. You tend to find casualties, drunken
> casualties, at the margins of these cultures. A lot of the
> Highlanders put out at the time of the Clearances ended
> up in places like Australia and promptly put the
> Aborigines out of their areas. So they in turn became
> tyrants. These are, of course, the paradoxes of history.

GAELIC AND CULTURAL SURVIVAL
THE SURVIVAL OF GAELIC (ICS Island)
> They have been saying for a large number of years that
> Gaelic is dying, that it is in a terminal condition. I can hardly
> see how a marginal language such as Gaelic can survive into
> a highly technological age, over the next century.

KEOSE, WHERE DERICK'S MATERNAL GRANDPARENTS
LIVED (ICS Bayble)
> We've come to Keose, which is important to Derick
> because of his ancestry here. It's just a little village at the
> side of Loch Erisort. There are a number of boats, and
> when we arrived we heard some children playing and

99

they were speaking in Gaelic and English and then their
mother came along and invited us up for a cup of coffee.

KEOSE, CHILDREN AND FAMILY HISTORY (DT Bayble)

Great to hear the young children with their mixture of
English and Gaelic song. My mother came from here and
her father belonged to a different part of Lewis, came
back from Glasgow with his recently married wife and
began looking for a site to build a house on; but at the
end of the day my grandfather had to build the house
right on the shore, with the waves continually lapping the
back wall. His workshop was at the back of the house. He
was among many other activities a joiner and coffin
maker. The house is still here, and I recognise the door
into the workshop.

THE POEM 'COFFINS' (DT Bayble)

The poem 'Coffins', it was not written until about thirty
years after my grandfather's death in the mid-Thirties
(1930s). What sparked off the writing of the poem was
the publication in 1963 of the 1961 Census figures for
Gaelic speakers, which showed quite a considerable drop
from previous census figures in 1951.

EXILE

EXILE (ICS Island)

It was there in Canada that I suddenly realised, in the stories
my old uncle was telling me, what exile meant in human
terms. He ran away from Lewis at the age of fourteen. He
ended up in Canada and he told me that lots of people he
had gone out with either starved to death or had become
alcoholics and there was a tremendous loss and wastage of
human talent in these periods; and I learned about the ships
that had left Lewis, and this, I think, sharpened for me the
idea of exile from the island.

LANGUAGE AND EXILE (ICS Island)

It's not so much exile from a particular place; it's exile
from a language, which is one of the really important

things. It forces you to confront linguistic things: whether in fact, if you were brought up speaking Gaelic and then transfer to writing in English, whether in fact your whole personality can emerge. I think of English and Gaelic as being a kind of bicycle, with a Gaelic wheel and an English wheel. Sometimes one is in operation and sometimes the other one is in operation; or the two of them manage to generate each other. The point is that when one talks about exile, one is not just talking about exile from a place, but also exile from a language; and as a poet is a person concerned with language, this is a question he has to consider very deeply.

THE POEM 'THE EXILES' (ICS Island)
That poem was started off by an image that remained in my memory of something my mother told me many, many years ago; and she said that there was this ship which was leaving Stornoway harbour, an immigrant ship, probably going to Canada, and at some particular point there was a spontaneous singing of psalms, so that the people on the ship and the people on the shore started singing 'The Lord's My Shepherd' as the ship moved away, and this was quite spontaneous. I always thought of that as an extremely moving experience. She said it was a very extraordinary and poignant moment.

CALLANISH
THE POEM 'AT THE STONES OF CALLANISH' (ICS Bayble)
Many people would probably consider Lewis to be a remote island, but lots of people from Lewis have been all over the world, and in this poem about Callanish, which is one of the main attractions of the island, the Callanish stone circle, I was trying to show this metaphor, a connection between Lewis and the outside world.

Three poets at Bayble

TAKING YOU HOME
POEMS BY ANDREW MITCHELL

Andrew Mitchell worked with Iain Crichton Smith on
The Island Is Always With You in 1988 as researcher,
interviewer and extracts editor for the final production.
He also went back to Lewis with Iain and Derick
Thomson in 1995 to make *How Many Miles From
Bayble?*, for which he had a similar research and
interview role. During this visit he became aware of
differences between the public and private responses of
both poets to the situation. Andrew began to explore the
poets' responses and the cultural issues of language,
community and religion. His own personal response took
the form of a twenty-four poem sequence, written
between 2002 and 2005, rather than a critical or
biographical study. The poet Myles Campbell has made
the translations into Gaelic.

"Carson a tha thu 'g iarraidh a dhol dhan àit' ud?"
Na faclan lom, an guth
ga dhìon fhèin mar gum biodh an cuireadh
air tighinn gun iarraidh

do shaoghal uaigneach, rud a bha.
Chùm mi orm a' còmhradh, an loidhne
a' cnagadaich: "Ach b' ann an sin a thòisich e uile
dhan dithis agaibh . . ."

'Why do you want to go to that place?'
The words stark, tone
defensive as though the invitation
had intruded upon

a private world, which it had. I resumed
the conversation, the line
crackling: 'But that was where it all began
for both of you . . .'

Steòrnabhagh

Sgiath plèan a' cromadh os cionn Ceann a Tuath Leòdhais,
san dealbh dhuinn tìr dhonn gun chraobh,
oirean a' triall air falbh; lochain le lòin,
breacadh chroitean is còmhnardan

farsaing de mhòintich dhuirche dhuinn
ag èirigh thugainn, gar crathadh
nar dùisg. Tarsainn rùm-fantainn beag
crathadh-làimhe is fàilte.

Seo e, stiùir-ghluasad anama, acarsaid
sheasgair, reul-iùil na cuimhne
bhon dealbhar seòl-mhap na beatha.
Soilleir, mionaideach, a' dorch-dheàrrsadh.

Stornoway

The plane wing dips over Northern Lewis, painting
a brown treeless landscape
with its trailing edge; puddled lochans,
a scattering of crofts and wide

expanses of dark brown moorland, which
lift towards us, jolt into
reality. Across the small departure lounge
handshakes and greetings.

This your steerageway of the soul, safe
anchorage, lode star of memory
from which the map of experience has been drawn.
Clear, precise and darkly shining.

Pabail

Muir gorm-uaine ri fhaicinn tro dhoras
briste seann taigh-tughaidh. Fuidheall
chabar ag èirigh, toirt dearg dhùbhlan dha na siantan.
An t-inneal a' tionndadh gu mall am measg muirinich,

a' cur arc-eòlas claistinneach an cèill, guthan
bho na seann làithean: gainmheach a' siabadh
don spàl 's e cur char 's na faoileagan a' sgreuchail gu h-àrd.
Seo cruth-tìre taibhseil, gun beò ann

ach triùir phàistean agus bàlla. Eathraichean
air an tarraing air tràigh san inntinn, lìn sgaoilte
son an càradh, seanchas air sgaothan a chailleadh
's a fhuaras. Feannagan lom nan tonn-ruith

chun na mara, an còmhdach ceilpe air iomall
cuimhne. Chan eil bàrr bhuntàta air iomair
a chaidh chruaidh-chladhach. Gun each, gun mhuc,
gun duine a' briseadh na sàmhchair, gun fheum air currac

a chur air coileach madainn Sàboinn. Hòl na chnocan
agus seirm a' chluig gan gairm
air ais dhan sgoil, casruisgt' fo cheilearadh na topaig
thig iad thairis an fheòir breac le dealt.

Bayble

Pale blue-green sea visible through the ruined
door of an old black house. Timber
remnants rise, rudely defiant against the elements.
The machine turns slowly amongst marram

grass, performs its auditory archaeology, voices
recount distant times: sand drifting
into the turning spool whilst gulls scream overhead.
This is a landscape of ghosts, inhabited

by three small children and a ball. Boats drawn
up in mind upon the beach, nets
spread for the mending with talk of shoals lost
and found. Lazy-beds rolling naked

towards the sea, their kelp covering a distant
memory. No flowering potato haulms
from hard dug earth. Silence not broken by horse,
pig or human, nor any need to hood

the cockerel before Sabbath morn. Hol now a hillock
as the chiming bell summons
them again to school, barefooted under the lark's song
they walk the dew-speckled grass.

Ròghadal

Muir soilleir le spotagan glas, sgòthan boga
os cionn nan cnoc. 'S mathaid gun do sheòl birlinn
a' Chinn-fheadhna a dh'eileanan eile air leithid de latha.
Mun cuairt air, iomairean air an àiteach, iasg a chaidh a ghlacadh,

beatha a' buan-dhannsa, na dusan
clàr-dhealbh fhèin, dùr-shnaidhte.
Os cionn mullach na h-altarach, far am biodh
ùrnaighean ag èirigh, tha tè làn-chumadail

a' riaghladh, braoisgeach, cìochan stòite
an aghaidh ghaothan is shruthan mara
agus leithid de ghal airson anman
a ghabh an cuan, a tha gu cian à sealladh.

Rodel

A clear sea, grey flecked with moist clouds hanging
over the hills. The Chief's galley
might have set sail for other isles on such a day.
About him, fields tilled, fish caught,

life dances on in its own sternly carved
twelve-panelled pictograph.
Above the chancel roof, where prayers
rose, an earlier voluptuary

presides, grins, thrusts forward breasts
against the sea winds and tides
and so much weeping for lost souls
sea-claimed and out of touch.

Deasbad

Chrath i a falt feamainn sruthanach
mara, agus a' tionndadh
thuirt i, "Chan eil eòlas ceart agad
ormsa." A malaidhean dùinte, deòir

sìos gruaidhean, fliuch mar mhol.
Ag osnaich, thàinig ris muineal
grinn, cho geal ri oitir.
I bàn, bilean mar ròs fiadhaich a-nis

druidte, dùinte; dealgan an fhacail
dhiùltaich a' tarraing am fala fhèin.
Gàirdeanan paisgte mar dhìon, sgòth
ìosal mun cuairt an dà chìch

bhinneanich bhig, cho teann ri
bàirnich air creagan oir a' chladaich.
An sin shuath siùil-mhara
na sliasaidean, 's a' cheò fhuar

gan còmhdach. Sùilean donn, cho geur
ri seabhag, a' gleidheadh an geur-amhairc
do-chreidsinn: a guth a' ghaoth:
"Cha bhi sibh an seo ach rè seal."

Dispute

She shook her streaming sea-
wrack hair, and turning
spoke, 'You don't really know
me.' Brows drawn, tears

falling over pebble wet cheeks.
Sighing, revealed a delicate
neck, white as sea-driven sand.
Pale, wild rose lips now

tightly closed; thorns of rejecting
words drawing their own
blood. Folded arms protective, low
cloud about the small, twin

peaked breasts, firm as limpet
shells on shoreline rocks.
There, tidal seas caressed her
thighs, whilst cold mist

covered them. Brown eyes, hawk
sharp, fix the disbelieving
stare: her voice the wind, 'You'll only
be here a short time.'

Cur an Cèill

Tha thu gar beagachadh bhod bhòrd-bhratha
àrd. Tha càraichean is coisichean san dol seachad
a' gabhail beachd air luach do chraicinn dhuinn.
Na sùilean domhainn èilde sin cho faileasach

ri muir chiùin fo ghrian an t-samhraidh. A-riamh mus
tog a' chiad topag i fhèin
gu neo-bhrìgh ann an èadhar shoilleir na maidne
tha mi air do mholadh, gus an glaodh

an lon-dubh deireannach beul na h-oidhche.
Goiridh sibh orm ann an seann
òrain: cho sùbailte ri eilid air creagan
corrach, mar a shiùbhlas leumadair-mara

àirde nan tonn copach, thig mi a laighe rid thaobh, na làmhan
fuaighte nad fhalt dualach dlùth,
cho teann ri fraoch fo fhlùr, a' fosgladh ar leabhair
làn aigheir is bròin.

Declaration

You dwarf us from your billboard height. Passing
cars and pedestrians
view the merits of your soft brown skin; those
deep doe eyes reflective

as a calm sea under summer sun. Before
the first lark lifts
itself to insignificance in the clear dawn air
I have praised you, until

the last blackbird heralds the dying light.
You call me in old
songs: agile as a young deer over craggy
rocks, as the dolphin crests

creamed waves, I come to lie beside you, hands
entwined in your close curled
hair, tight as flowering heather, opening our book
of such delights and sorrows.

Taigh-solais

Muir an earraich, drùidhteach le solas
agus coibhneil fo chlòimh ghil nan sgòth.
An tìr aon-dathach donn, lom mar deic bàta
ro stoirm a' gheamhraidh: croitean

an cargu màbte. Rubha is tràigh, dìdean
an aghaidh nan seachd siantan.
Cho finealta àrd, an taigh-solais ag èirigh so-ghointe
mar mhnaoi a' feitheamh tilleadh

dhachaigh fir, bràthar no mic. Creideamh a solas-iùil –
mòr-phàirt doimhneachd do-chreidsinneach
mara is earbsa, far a bheil beatha uaireannan na gibht
aig tionndadh sruthanach sgal gaoithe.

Lighthouse

Spring sea, light infused and benign beneath
its fleece cloud covering. A brown
monotoned landscape clear as any ship's deck
against winter storms: crofts the battered

cargo. Headland and beach bulwark
against elemental forces.
Elegantly tall, the lighthouse rises vulnerable
as a woman waiting the return

of husband, brother, son. Faith her beacon,
so much a part of the unfathomable
depths of sea and belief, where survival sometimes
rests on the eddying turn of a squall.

A' Tadhal

Dh'iarr am muir a thadhal

Chan eil e gu diofar dè bheir thu leat: lìon,
loidhne, cliabh-ghiomach, lìon-sguabaidh.
Bidh an aon fhàilte romhad. Caochladh
fhonn – bho lochan ciùin

air latha samhraidh gu dearg chuthach
thar chuthach clann nan daoine:
sin uile ann an uair an uaireadair. Na feuch
ri thomhas 's tu a' cruaidh-shlaodadh

's a' tarraing gus a bhogadh; 's dìomhain dhut.
'S na feuch tomhas eile
's tu dèanamh air cladach, a' taghadh
fèath, às dèidh thonnan

gan cunntadh. Bi cinnteach às, bidh gach pàirt
dhed bhodhaig bog, air a sgioladh
le sàl agus brùite. Bidh gach turas
air leth; cha tig thu

gu bràth air dhà co-ionann.
Air dhut tilleadh, agus tadhal
air do nàbaidh, bidh 's dòcha grèim
bìdh èisg ann, no 's dòcha gun ith iad thusa.

Visiting

The sea wants to be visited

What you take does not matter: net,
line, lobster pot or trawl.
There'll be the same welcome. Moods
vary from a still lochan

on a summer's day to black rage
beyond the fury of human
kind: often in the same hour. Don't
try to guess as you heave

and haul to launch; it's no use.
Or try to second-guess
on your run for shore, picking
stillness, after numbered

waves. Expect every part of your
body to be wet, salt
raw and bruised. Each visit
is unique, one of those

never to be repeated experiences.
On return, after visiting
your neighbour, there may be a meal
of fish, or they may eat you.

Iolaire

Muir coibhneil, critheanach le tuinn bheaga eagarra,
ann an grèin chaoin an earraich.
Chan eil am bàgh beag ach mar lùbadh
san oirthir, gu far a bheil corrag

a' cur an cèill, "Sin far an deach i sìos."
Chan eil comharra, no clàr a dhìth,
cuimhne sluaigh a' cumail slàn
na Callainn ud, Naoi-deug –

naoi-deug, còrr 's dà cheud seòladair
a' tilleadh dhachaigh bhon chogadh, mòran dhiubh
a sheòl air marannan nach fhaigh thu
ann an atlas sgoile, a shiab

air acair aig an spot seo: teaghlaichean cho faisg
's gum faodadh iad èigheach ri chèile, tiodhlacan
paisgte, an dùil tighinn còmhla. Gus na dhùisg
spùtan-mara na doimhneachd

nan dearg chuthach, agus chaidh i thairis.
Air an tilgeil len tiodhlacan
air an tuil, muinntir baile a' togail cuid a chaidh fhàgail
bog le sàl shìos fo na taighean.

Iolaire

A benign sea, rippling with small regular waves,
gentle in spring sunshine.
The small bay no more than a curve
in the coastline, where a finger

points, 'That's where she went down.'
No marker, no plaque needed,
a collective memory which keeps
that Hogmanay, Nineteen-

nineteen, when over two hundred sailors
returning home from war, many
having sailed on seas not marked
upon a school atlas, swung

overnight at anchor on this spot: families
within hailing distance, presents
wrapped, reunion anticipated. Until
the sea spouts of the deep

opened and in their fury, she foundered.
Cast with their presents upon
the surge, villagers lifting some washed
sea-sodden on their home beach.

Ceòs

Gann de dh'àite airson togail, dh'èirich
an taigh eadar rathad is muir. An làn a' srùthladh ris a' bhalla-cùil,
chunntadh e na bha sa phost, dhèanadh e

na cisteachan-laighe, lem brèid Beurla. Taigh
nan òran. An-diugh tha a' chlann a' cluich
nan dithis, a' measgachadh's a' maidseadh
an abairtean, a' toirt òran an drungair

gu ruige a' mhaic, mus tèid sinn airson teatha. An taigh seo
cuairtichte le craobhan: air an cur aon Sàboinn
le dotair Sasannach trithead bliadhna air ais.
"Iadsan a bha feitheamh fearg an Uile-chumhachdaich,

tha iad air a bhith feitheamh fada. 'S e an àirde
a chuireas às dhaibh," canaidh ar neach-aoigheachd,
an coire ri crònan 's na muasgain-chaola spàg-shìnte
anns an t-sinc, a' feitheamh ri baisteadh

an fhìor-uisg'. "Cha do dh'ionnsaich an duine agam,
iasgair Sasannach, a-riamh an cànan. Tha sinn modhail
na chuideachd, gun ach a' bheag ga ràdh. A' chlann-nighean?
Tha a' Ghàidhlig aca bhon caraidean."

Keose

Destitute of a place to build, the house
rose between the road and sea.
High tide lapping against the back wall
where he counted the post, made

coffins with their 'English' braid. A home
of singing. Today the children play
two-handed, mix and match their phrases,
add a Gaelic drunkard's song

to the mike, before we go for tea. This house
surrounded by trees: Sabbath-planted
by an English doctor thirty years before.
'Those waiting for the Almighty's wrath

have had a long wait. Their height will be
their undoing,' our host adds,
the kettle singing as Dublin Bay prawns sprawl
in the sink, await their freshwater

baptism. 'My English, fisherman husband
never learned the language. We're polite
in his presence, barely speak a word. The girls?
They have the Gaelic from their friends.'

Fuadachadh
Cuiridh mi às an fhearann thu

Ann an solas na moch-maidne 's an coileach
a' gairm air croit pìos bhuaithe
thàinig iad air a thòir: spìon iad an doras
fosgailte ann an cabhaig, a' bàthadh

an teine meadhan làir. An oidhche ron sin
dh'inns e seann sgeulachd
dhan chloinn an sin, 's an uair sin
sheinn e òran ro àm dol a laighe.

Dh'èirich i bho phoit-teatha na bracaist. Tharraing i
a' chlann làn eagail gu a
dreasa 's ghlaodh i nach bu chòir dhaibh
am mullach a thoirt bhon taigh.

Iad uile gan coimhead a' gearradh nan sìoman fraoich, tughadh
donn 's an uair sin dubh a' dòrtadh
sìos gu talamh. A' briseadh
nan cabar mar a ghluais iad

gus an robh e uile làn-fhosgailte dhan speur; am beul
fosgailte, tron tàinig
sgread na gaoith, agus fhaclan gu follaiseach
sgrìobhte le sùith air a' bhalla,

"Seo cho fad' 's a thèid dol sìos na Gàidhlig."
Ghabh e dà thaobhan ceangailte
's thog e air a ghualainn iad
fa chomhair feumalachd. Sguab i

Eviction

I shall evict you from the land

In the early morning light as the cock
crowed on a nearby croft
they came for him: wrenched the door
open in haste, drowned

the central fire. The previous night
he had told an old
tale to the children there, then sang
a song before bedtime.

She rose from the breakfast pot. Clutched
frightened children to her
skirts and screamed they should not
take the roof from this house.

All watched heather ropes cut, brown
then black thatch cascading
down upon the ground. Breaking roof
timbers as they went

until the whole was exposed to sky; open-
mouthed, through which
wind howled, and his words written
visibly in soot on the wall,

'This is as far as the Gaelic decline goes.'
He took up two joined cross
timbers, heaved them on his shoulder
against chance use. She swept

thuice an leanabh a b' òige 's an t-aodach-
leapa tana, chùm i grèim teann
air làimh tèile, agus lean an treas fear
a' glaodhaich air a cùl. Throm-cheumnaich iad gu sàmhach

air falbh, an cinn crom; coimeasgte le
cruth-tìre a' mhonaidh, 's fios aca nach ann
san t-saoghal seo an sealbh, fhad 's a rinn a' bhò
a dh'fhàg iad geum, ag iarraidh bleoghan.

up the youngest child with the flimsy
bedding, held another tightly
by the hand, whilst a third, wailing, followed
on behind. They trudged silently

away, heads down; merged into moorland
landscape, knowing their
kingdom was never of this world, whilst the cow
they left bellowed for milking.

Sàboinn

Tur-shàmhchair. Nàdar cha mhòr balbh
ach na sailm fad' às
ag èirigh gu flaitheas air an t-soirbheas. Am muir
a' srùthladh ris an oitir-bacaidh, fhad 's a leughar

an leadan searbh airson nam mìltean de mhnathan
a' saothrachadh fo mhàbadh dìmeasach
ann am puirt chèin. Tha a leithid fhaireachdainn,
a leithid bròn sàile a' co-dhaingneachadh

fonn fad' às fear togail fuinn. Ach fhathast,
leth-cheud bliadhna às dèidh a thriall,
tha an leughadair a' cromadh, a' feòrach math dh'fhaodte
an cluinneadh duine a ghuidhe airson ceartas.

Sabbath

Silence absolute. Nature almost stilled
except for the distant psalms
lifting heavenwards on the breeze. Sea
lapping the breakwater as the bitter

litany is read for so many thousand women
working under the abusive disdain
of distant ports. Such feeling, such salt
water sorrow counterpoints

the distant cantor's rising tone. Yet still,
fifty years after departure,
the reader crouches, inquires if anyone
might have heard his plea for justice.

Còmhradh

Choisich e air an t-slighe
leotha, eadar an Cnoc
is Garrabost. Chriathraich e
am faclan mar dhuine a' lorg

ùir mìn airson cur. Shaoil iad
gur ceistear e,
gu h-àraidh nuair shuidh iad nan triùir
airson greis air an talamh

dhonn-uaine, agus b' ann air tròcair
agus creideamh a chailleadh a bhruidhinn e.
Rinn dithis bhoireannach strì
thar boglach mòna fhad 's a

shuidh iad. Na clèibh throm, làn
mòna, agus an dromannan
crùbte mar chruth-ìomhaigh
de chreutairean sgiathach

a' strì gus èirigh. Chaidh fraoch
faisg orra a lasadh.
Èiridh ceò an àirde 's iad
a' dealachadh. Aon le smuain

na choiseachd, air a' Bhràigh, mar
a dh'fhaodadh na mairbh nam ballachan
a bhith feitheamh an Ierusalem nuaidh.
Sin mar a chuala an sinnsear

Conversation

He walked along the way with
them, between Knock
and Garrabost. Sifted their
words as a man wanting

fine soil for planting. A catechist
they took him for,
especially when all three sat
a while on the brown-green

earth, and his words were on
mercy and lost faith.
Two women struggled over
the peat bog whilst

they sat. Heavy creels full
of peats and bent
backs profiled their shapes
as winged creatures

struggling to fly. Heather close
by had been fired.
Smoke drifting upwards at their
parting. One thinking

as he walked, on the Braighe, how
the walled-in dead
might await the New Jerusalem.
So their ancestors heard

aig na coinneamhan mòra, a' tighinn còmhla
mar sgaoth chudaigean
ris a' chladach. Am feasgar sin, fhad 's a
chaidh an fhalaisg na caoir

dh'èalaidh a chorrag tarsainn nam facal,
stad air eadar cinnt
agus teagamh. 'S a' ghaoth ag èirigh,
smaoinich e orrasan aig muir, seasmhach

nan dreuchd, a' stiùireadh cùrsa
tro mhuir bagarrach
mus ruig iad tìr, eadar an Cuan Sgìth
is cladach Chanàain.

at the great gatherings, collecting
like a shoal of cuddies
on the shore. That evening, whilst
the heather blazed,

his fingers crept across the words,
halting between certainty
and doubt. As winds rose, he
imagined those at sea hold

their posts, steering a course
through rising seas
to landfall, between the Minch
and Canaan's shore.

Peacadh

Ciont ag èaladh. Faireachadh fo thalmhainn
cho cinnteach ri gearradh glan
na mòna. Bheir thu 'n aire gu bheil e ann
a cheart cho furasta ri sin, chì thu a chumadh.

E ann cho cinnteach ris an stòl air an tug
am ministear oirre suidhe. Ise pròiseil,
chan ainmicheadh i athair, mar sin
dh'fhàg e oirre gun robh i ri siùrsachd

ann an sgìre eile. Cha robh tairbh an àite
math gu leòr. Dh'fhan i
na tost, ag imeachd a Ghlaschu
gu beatha air aineol. Abair glaodh

's an càr a' dol seachad:
"Sin taigh a' Pheacaich!"
An dithis ag aontachadh, agus air ceist
a chuid peacaidh, an fhreagairt, "A h-uile càil!"

Abair thusa roghainnean san amharc:
deoch, boireannaich, drogaichean, caoraich?
Mar gum biodh a chruth air fleòdradh ann an
ceò bhuidhe mharbh, gu sàmhach air aineol.

Sin

Guilt lurks. A subterranean feeling
certain as a clear cutting
of the peat. You can mark its presence
as easily, note its shape.

Real as the milking stool the Minister
made her sit upon. Proud,
she would not name the father, so he
accused her of going whoring

in another parish: the local bulls
not good enough. She held
her silence, departing then for Glasgow
and a life in exile. Such

sudden exclamation as the car passed:
'That's the Sinner's house!'
Affirmed by both and on the question
of his sins the reply, 'Everything!'

Left the mind agape with possibilities:
drink, women, drugs, sheep?
He seemed to float outlined in a yellow
glassy haze, soundlessly alien.

Cutadh

An t-seàla air a tarraing dlùth
mu guailnean an aghaidh
fuachd na maidne. Corragan air an còmhdach
le stiallan aodaich gus nach measgaich

a fuil leis an fhuil a tha mu thràth
air a' bhòrd cutaidh. Sgadan na laighe
rag le shùil ghlainne, cruaidh-
chruth, lannan air liathadh. Sgian

os a chionn; sgrìobhaidh i aon loidhne dhearg
air a' bhrù
a tha bòcadh: a' magadh air na lannan
trìd-shoilleir, cho lìonmhor ris na faclan

a lìonas faclair. Ceann, earball agus cnàimh-droma
nan gràmar de ghluasad
ioma-lùbach droma, air an caitheamh: gun
an còrr bhreab seòlta bhon earball,

cho clis ri gin a liric. Mionach 's eachdraidh
na chnàmhadh air an tilgeil gu na faoileagan
sgriachach, fhad 's tha na bloighean èisg
aig fois, sàmhach anns na baraillean reòthte.

Gutting

The shawl drawn close about her
shoulders against early
morning chill. Fingers bound with thin
cloth strips prevent her blood

mingling with that already settled
on the gutting table. Glass-
eyed and prone a herring lies, stiff-
lined, scales faded. Knife

poised, she pens a single red line
upon the distended
belly: mockery of translucent
scales, numerous as words

filling a dictionary. Head, tail and spine
a grammar of sinuous
dorsal movement, lifted away: no
more subtle tail flicks

clever as any lyric. Entrails, digestive
history thrown to bickering
gulls, whilst fillets rest disembodied,
silent in iced barrels.

Dùn Chàrlbhaigh

Cuairt-thrannsa eadar ballachan
co-shìnte a' tionndadh gu mall an àirde
toirt sealladh fuar on uchd-bhalla. Innleachdach
's dlùth-dhèante, Prionnsa Cruithneach

a' togail ri aghaidh ionnsaigh nan Sgot. A' cleachdadh
a sgilean gus a theaghlach a chumail beò, ainmean
chnoc, aibhnichean, pholl-mara a ghleidheadh, seann sgeul
is uirsgeul a shnìomh air an fhearann mun chagailt

gheamhraidh. Seo cridhe a mhiann,
seiche-dhùbailte, clach-chinnteach.
Bho uchd-bhalla briste sgapaidh na croitean a-mach,
iathairean a' deàrrsadh mar chlaidheamhan sa ghrèin.

Dun Carloway

A circuitous passage between parallel
walls turns slowly upwards
for a cold parapet view. Ingenious
and compact, a Pictish prince

building against invading Scots. Using his skills
to keep family alive, retain names
of hills, rivers, stretches of sea, weave myths
and legends into landscape round winter

fires. This was the centre of his desires,
double-skinned, assured in stone.
From its broken parapet the crofts spread out,
aerials gleam like swords in the sun.

Brèinis

Rathad gun cheann-uidhe, a' stad gu h-obann
sna dùin ghainmhich. Neònach, gun stadadh
cuibhreann innleadaireachd slànachaidh
ann am fàsach feòir air a shiabadh

le gaineimh. "Dìreach eaconamas," togaidh cuideigin
's sinn a' fàgail a' chàir. "Theirig
an t-airgead. Bha fir an urra ris an rathad sheachranach seo
airson an dòil . . ." Dh'inns crathadh guailne

na dh'fheumte 's sinn a' teàrnadh chun na tràighe gil. Torran
a dh'ionnlaid an Cuan Siar ag èirigh mar bhasalt
dubh, eileanan rag righinn a' toirt dùbhlan
do dh'onfhadh tìm.

Brenish

A road going nowhere halts suddenly
in sand dunes. Illogical a piece
of therapeutic engineering should end
in a wilderness of sand-blown

grasses. 'Pure economics,' someone adds
as we leave the car. 'The money
ran out. Men relied on this wandering road
for their dole . . .' A shrug of the shoulders

says all as we descend to white sands. Atlantic-
sifted, stacks rising basalt
black, stubbornly resistant islands defy
the surge of time.

Eilthireachd

O, 's làidir na bannan tha 'm tharraing a-null
Gu eilean beag donn MhicLeòid;
Gun stiùirinn gun solas do d'chala mo long
Nuair ruigeas mi ceann mo lò.

Dòmhnall Moireasdan

Beò bliadhnaichean à ceas: rumannan
ma làimh, bothain
le bobhstairean connlaich air an tarraing
suas gu stòbhaichean ceòthach. Madaidhean-allaidh

a' donnalaich a-muigh mar spioradan caillte, a' toirt
tìr eile gu cuimhne. Tro mhìltean
sàmhach mòr-choille tha mac-talla
làmhaigh, air a mheasgadh

le guthan, balaich à bailtean eile san Eilean. Le turchairt
a' coinneachadh ann am bàr; còmhradh
oidhche fhuar gheamhraidh air an dachaigh, drama
a' toirt blàth-fhaireachdainn do chuimhne.

An litir chrìon bhuidhe dheireannach bho phàrantan:
goirid, aithghearr mar an anail
a' fàillinn, ga gleidheadh mar a thèid còrd-imleig
glas an uisge-stiùrach a ghearradh bhon Eilean.

Exile

Oh, strong are the ties that draw me over
to MacLeod's little brown isle;
I could steer my vessel without a light to harbour
when my days come to an end.

Donald Morrison

Years of life from a suitcase: doss-
house rooms, cabins
with palliases drawn close to black
smoking stoves. Wolves

howling outside like lost spirits, evoking
another land. Through
silent miles of still forest the axe
resounds, mixed with

voices, boys from other island villages. Chance
meetings in bars; cold
winter night talk of home, whisky
adding sentiment to memory.

That last faded yellow letter from parents:
short, abrupt as failing
breath, held as the grey umbilical wake
severs from the isle.

Calanais

Clach-cheangail bhiorach, a' gràbhadh an adhair anns an
dian-ghaoith fhuar. Lochan glas agus Iain a' leughadh
mu mhurt leanaibh, oidheam air Hiroshìma
sa bhliadhna cuimhneachaidh.

Àite suirghe far an cuimhnich Ruaraidh
bhith raighdeadh baidhc agus cuirmean-cnuic air làithean
fada samhraidh. Fuachd a' tàthadh corrag is camara,
gorm san dùil-fheitheamh,

cuideam gach fir air a' phrìomh chloich, gun chùram,
furasta leis a' chùis,
fhad 's tha fear le bonaid chlòimh 's *theodolite*
's falbhan air air sgàth ceart-cheàrnan.

An tig faclan beò à slighe nan clach? An càrn
sinn iad gu pongail
an aghaidh na mòmaid nuair nach bi duine an seo
le anail, ach nam mac-talla den t-sàmhchair sa?

Callanish

Keystone sharp, etching the sky in a biting
cold wind. Lochs grey as Iain
reads of child murder, hints at Hiroshima
in the anniversary year.

A place of courtship where Derick remembers
cycle rides and picnics on long
summer days. Cold fuses finger and camera,
blue with anticipation,

as each leans against the keystone, nonchalant,
at ease with the moment,
whilst a woolly-hatted man with a theodolite
fusses over precise angles.

Can words survive the way of stones? Shall
we heap them precisely
against the moment when all here no longer
breathe, but echo this silence?

A' Cuimhneachadh

A' laighe air lèana, am measg feur
milis, oiteag chaoin
a' tionndadh gud ghuth, gu socair a' cunntadh
rionnagan samhraidh. Thu suas

dlùth rium, tha fàileadh mòna ùir dhiot:
suathadh caomh a' cur fadachd
san fheòil. Cogais a' moladh
gach gnìomh: ceilpe air iomairean

chaidh dhroch thionndadh; buntàta, arbhar is eòrna
air an cur. Samh sa bhàthaich fhathast
de chàth air a bruich, braich
airson a' bho a chumail tron

gheamhradh. Do speal fhathast na stob,
peannan meirgeach donn,
's am machair gun spealadh on dh'fhàg thu.
'S dòcha gun do chruinnich thu

sìol, gun tug thu leat crom-lusan nan spotag dubha
's iad gnogadh, gan sgapadh
thairis crèadh fhuar dhorch Fhlannrais
far a bheil thu nis sìnte.

Remembering

Lying upon the meadow, amongst sweet
grasses, a gentle breeze
becomes your voice, softly counting
summer stars. Firm

against me, you smell of new peats:
gentle touch making
a body ache. Conscience lists each
task: kelp on poorly

dug beds; potatoes, oats and barley
planted. The byre reeking
yet of boiled chaff, malty mash
to keep the cow through

winter. Still your scythe confronts,
brown rusting pennant,
the machair not cut since you left.
Perhaps you gathered

seeds, took nodding black-eyed poppies
with you, scattering
them over the cold dark clay of Flanders
where you now lie.

Air Fhighe

Air ungadh an aghaidh na gaoithe, uisge agus gnìomhan
ciontach, ciamar a ghabhas an t-aodach seo
a rèiteach, ach le cluaran, ionnsramaid
leabhar nan ceist – a' sgaradh

caoraich Shàboinn bho na gobhair? Tha an sluagh seo air a bhith ro fhada
nam fiaclan an leòmhainn, geur-ghreimeach, duileasg
ruadh raineachail, ronnach bho am bilean – sàcramaid
fala ìmpireil. Cuigeal a chaoidh

air a sgaradh eadar àiteachas is dualchas, uachdaran
is cànan; co-chothrom cugallach
gun bharantas eadar còir-fearainn is cainnt.
A' chagarsaich ud thar chlachan nathrach,

cuimhne a' ruith luath-ghleusta tro an dannsa
le searbhachd à taighean
millte, a thàinig air gaoth nam fuadach. A dh'aindeoin
an rèidh-ghlagadaich, tha an spàl-fhighe

bhith dèanamh phàtranan umhail a' dùsgadh shamhan
a tha 'g iarraidh an anairt ghil bhaistidh fhèin
gus droch aislingean a chiùineachadh agus an rìoghachd ud
air bheil aithris. Tha am bòrd ullamh, tionndaidhidh

gach tè a tha na h-àite deiseil: làmh dheas le brag
sìos gu clì, òrain mar chlaidheamhan
cruaidhe, freumh seileastair gorm an aghaidh luchd-amhairc.
Crathadh corraige cromaidh cho eagarra

ri gin a chunntas-sluaigh. Eadar bhith na bhanais
is taigh-fhaire, tha an roile thioram seo
a' cur bois air rudhadh òigheil, mus dèan i oidhirp seasamh
saor o bhòrd, deiseil is beannaichte.

Woven

Anointed against wind, rain and acts of bad
conscience, how shall this fabric
be teased out, except with a thistle, instrument
of catechism, separating Sabbath

sheep from goats? These people have been the lion's
teeth too long, sharp biting, red
fronded dulse drools from their lips in a sacrament
of Imperial blood. Distaff always

cleft between cultivation and culture, landlord
and language; precarious balance
without certainty of tenure or speech. Those
whisperings over snake stones,

memories running swift-fingered through their dance
with bitterness from broken
houses, brought upon winds of clearance. Despite
the even rattle, being shuttled

into conforming patterns brings pungent odours
requiring their own white, baptismal
linen to appease bad dreams and that other talked
of kingdom. The board is set, all

in their place shall turn with the sun: right
dashed down left, songs steeled
as swords, blue iris root against onlookers.
Wagging middle finger accurate

as any census. Somewhere between a wedding
and a wake, this dried windage
palms virginal blushes, before attempting to stand
stick free, sun turned and blessed.

Air feadh an tùir-fhaire

Air cùl globa beag lom solas a sheòmair-chadail,
tha Dougie a' leum 's a' bocail,
na fhaileas dorcha a' mùthadh dòrainn
an inneil làn-fhuaime: a' cluich a ghiotàr

leis a' chearraig agus bun-os-cionn, mar ùmhlachd
do a ghaisgeach, Hendrix. Boile rabhdach
eileagtronaigeach agus iadsan nan loidhne ris
an drochaid ìosal ag èisteachd, an tacsa

an uchd-bhalla, air an cur iad botail pop,
a' crac air dè as àirde sna clàir.
Siabaidh sèist Dhougie sa chiaradh os cionn
sùmainn a' Chuain Siar fhad 's tha Sheanair,

beul fosgailte le srann, ga gharadh ri teine
a' chidsin, a' pìochanaich os cionn a' mheileòidian
sàmhach na uchd, cho stòlda ri cat dubh na chadal:
a-rithist an drochaid faramach, fo ruitheam

siùbhlach a bhogsa, cnapadh nan cas.
Aon uair eile, tha Moira gu beadarrach
ga thoirt fo sgàil an iomair na h-asbhuain, fo
ghealaich shoillsich an fhoghair, gu sàmhach

ga chuairteachadh ann am blàths a bodhaig,
cho maoth ris a' chonnlaich anns a bheil iad
nan laighe, ga chòmhdach le pògan fliucha
gus an dùisg e, le aon srann mhòr.

All along the watchtower

Behind the small bare bulb of his bedroom
light, Dougie leaps and prances,
a dark shadow modulating the anguished
amplifier: his guitar played

left-handed and upside down in homage
to his hero, Hendrix. A frenzied
electronic rant, listened to by those lining
the low bridge, leaning against

its parapet, where they place pop bottles,
discuss the latest chart-toppers.
Dougie's dusk chorus drifts above Atlantic
swell whilst his grandfather

snores open-mouthed, warmed by the kitchen
fire, wheezing over lap-
silent melodeon, still as a sleeping black cat:
again the bridge resounds, beneath

the fluid rhythm of his squeeze-box drumming
feet. Once more, Moira coaxes
into the darkness of the stubbled field, under
glowing autumn moon, silently

envelopes him in the warmth of her body,
soft as the straw they lie
on, covers him in wet kisses until,
with one large snore, he wakes.

A' Bhàsa

I seo, bhàsa d' Eilein loma-làn,
thu cuimhneachadh d' òige:
as t-earrach, feadagan a' neadachadh
's a' chiad ghearradh den mhòine.

As t-samhradh, feur sa chruaich san àm
nuair a chuireas an traon a' ghrian a chadal.
As t-fhoghar, dannsa nan gèadh fiadhaich,
cumaidhean eagarra gu h-àrd.

Sa gheamhradh, a' ghaoth a' tilgeil nam faoileag
mun adhar, cuitheachan sneachda. Glèidhte,
tobar dhomhainn na cuimhne
a' caomh-chumail, ri aghaidh

dhrisean a thig le tìm. An còta-glainne soilleir,
cumaidhean daingeann: anail
neo-chaochlaideach an coileantachd. Foisdineach
anns a' mhòmaid nuair

a chumas sùilean laga, silteach
am fòcas preasach air saoghal nas ùire,
's caochlaideach. Fòghnadh – turas gu
mòr-bhùth ann an Steòrnabhagh: croitean

sàmhach, falamhachd achadh is oir cladaich
nam fianais air an atharrachadh seo.
Eilthireachd, às-imrich gu tìrean cèin
air cunnradh dà bhliadhna.

Fhad 's a sheirmeas na raointean-cluiche le Beurla,
cainnt an telebhisein
agus a' chosnaidh, seargaidh a' Ghàidhlig
gu bhith na cuspair roghnach.

The Vase

This, your island vase replete
with childhood memories:
Spring, nesting plovers and first
cutting of the peat.

Summer, hay stooked when corncrakes
serenade the sunset.
Autumn, dancing with wild geese
flying formations overhead.

Winter, gulls blown about the sky
and drifting snow. All fixed,
held dear in the deep wellspring
of memory, against briars

time brings. This glaze clear,
figures distinct: breath
of their perfection unchanging. Stilled
at the moment when

weakened, watery eyes hold their
webbed focus on a newer,
changing world. Sufficiency, a supermarket
run to Stornoway: silent

crofts, emptiness of field and foreshore
witness this change.
Emigration, a flight to foreign parts
on a two year contract.

Whilst playgrounds resonate with English,
language of television
and employment, Gaelic atrophies
to a subject choice.

Slàn

Chaidh thu dhachaigh gu eilean do
mhic-meanmna, thog thu
dòrlach ùir, chriathraich thu smaointean, agus suidhidh tu
air tulach inntinn, ann an sàmhchair fosaidh.

Suarach an fhàilte a bh' ort a' tighinn dhachaigh:
bu bheag a bh' ann de chruachan-mòna
aig an doras los gun cuimhnicheadh tu na seann
dòighean, 's chaidh do thaigh

atharrachadh. An rùm san lobhta dhorch ud
far an suidheadh tu, far na dh'fhàs mac-meanmna,
a-nis le uinneagan mòra dormair,
gun mheang, deàrrsach 's làn solais.

Gu socair air an oiteig thig fuaim
dannsa an fhoghair, fuaim air fhuaim
air an drochaid fhiodha, 's gu h-àrd,
tha do rogha gealaich foghair a' riaghladh.

Mar a sgapas an lasair sna speuran
tuigidh mi airson a' chiad uair
nach eil thu air camhanaich fhaicinn. Nam chluais
tha am muir meallta a' briseadh

a-rithist air cladach Phabail, a' ghaoth bhiorach
gheur, garg-gheal tha beanntan Chataibh
a' deàlradh, 's ceilearadh nan eun
nam cheann 's mi smèideadh slàn leibh.

Farewell

You have gone home to the island of your
imagination, lifted a handful
of soil, sifted ideas, and sit upon a hillock
of the mind, in undisturbed quiet.

Your homecoming was not so welcoming:
there were few peat stacks
at the door to remember the old ways
by, and your house had been

converted. That dark loft space in which
you sat, where imagination grew,
now boasts large dormer windows,
pristine, bright and full of light.

Faintly upon the breeze comes the sound
of the autumn dance, resonant
on the wooden bridge; above, your
favourite autumn moon presides.

As the spreading blazure fills the sky
I am conscious for the first time
that you have not seen the dawn. In
my ear the deceptive sea breaks

again upon Bayble shore, wind stinging
sharp, harshly white Sutherland
mountains glisten, the birds singing
in my head as I wave farewell.

Keose visit
Back row: Julian May, Iain Crichton Smith, Derick Thomson and
Tina Carrington
Front row: Anne Macleod with Eve, Jo and Eilidh Carrington